THE FINAL INTERLUDE
Advancing Age and Life's End

Lee Roloff
&
Russell Lockhart

THE LOCKHART PRESS
Everett, Washington

Copyright © 2016

Lee Roloff and Russell Lockhart

ISBN 978-0-911783-07-0

Cover Image

"Pondering" by Russell Lockhart (2008)
Black and white rendering of
oil-swabbed cotton on heavy 9 x 12 linen paper

DEDICATION

It is only with age
that you acquire the gift
to evaluate decay,
the epiphany of Wordsworth,
the wisdom of wabi-sabi:
nothing is perfect,
nothing is completed,
nothing lasts.

—*Paul Theroux*

…and I hear what Lee might have said:

Except memory;
if not mine, yours;
if not yours, others'
—*hopefully.*

TABLE OF CONTENTS

FOREWORD

Russell Lockhart

My friend, colleague, and co-author, Lee Roloff, died on October 5, 2015. We had just completed the manuscript of *The Final Interlude: Advancing Age and Life's End.* I had hoped I could put a finished copy of the book in Lee's hands before I would have to write a forward such as this.

It was not to be.

Lee had insisted I be listed as the first author, but I never agreed to this. *The Final Interlude* was Lee's idea, or more accurately, his dream's idea. The dream came with the full title: *The Final Interlude: Advancing Age and Life's End.* We changed the title several times, but I have here set the title back to what the dream announced. It was Lee's continuing passion for the material and enthusiastic responses he would receive from audiences when he presented lectures on this most difficult theme that kept the project alive. He was deeply immersed in the experience of the final interlude with all its torments, travails, impossibilities; yet, he caught hold of all the glistening twinkles of life yet to be lived in whatever final time he had. Those who knew Lee will know why I use the word "twinkle."

I have left the main text unchanged after we completed this work. It does not reflect the fact that Lee has died. I did not want to change anything he had written or said to reflect this. I send it into the world as it was when he was alive. I will miss our lunches, our phone calls, our emails. Those varied times together were always full of sparks between us and we left those encounters refreshed and rejuvenated and enlivened with ideas and potentials. He was a guide to me in how to live in the final interlude which I now approach with a kind of loving attitude which he embodied and made real. I hope his words here will have that effect on readers as well. I would like that. He would have liked it too.

Russell Lockhart
Everett, Washington
October 7, 2015

INTRODUCTION

"Those who only says what is truth,
they're not worth listening to."
*The 100-Year-Old Man Who Climbed
Out the Window and Disappeared*
Jonas Jonasson,
quoting his grandfather

It is fall 2015. Lee was 88 in August. Russ will be 77 in November. We are getting on, aging, growing *old*. We are "over the hill," going down the other side toward the "valley of the shadow of death." Each in our own way, we are in or approaching the "final interlude." Along the way, losses mount: friends, functions, capacities. Still, we have not yet lost our minds, our memories are available, the creative spark remains alive and well and we have sparked one another to engender what follows.

We have not produced a scholarly essay on aging from the Jungian perspective as might be expected from two aging Jungian analysts. Rather, we present a potpourri, an assemblage, a collage of snippets from memories that came forward, interview portraits of others, some still here, some gone, and conversations we've had on what occurs to us, as we mull and contemplate what lies before us, what comes after the final interlude. We have been free to do what we want, to play, as it were, giving full expression to "lude" (from L. *ludus*, "play"), to follow the path leading to the inevitable. The shoulds and oughts of earlier times no longer tug, what others think no longer of concern. Our joy lies in being able to express at all.

REFLECTIONS

Lee Roloff

Portraits of Individuals in the Final Interlude

Meditating and writing about "the final interlude" in *my* final interlude of life's journey
has its poignancy to be sure. While my body moves
in slower rhythms, my mind and its imaginative
powers paradoxically produce energies that promote
a new psychological awakening in me. My career is
over, my pursued achievements attained, my progeny
now caring for their father, and my constant "view"
is forward—to the conclusion of my life. "What
has been" is now in the realm of memory. "What is
to be" is in the unfolding of each new day. In the
earlier stages of my life, each stage had its goals of
achievements in the world. In the final interlude,
I realize my life task is to live as fully as I am able,
while developing an acute and ever present awareness of the coming final moments—my end.

I know that the *education* of psyche is first in its
essences and the acceptance of its facts. The first

13

fact is the exteriorities of life, and the second fact is the interiorities of life. I have reckoned with each of these two vast domains in my own individual ways as each of us must. C.G. Jung, in his late reflections observed, "I try to see the line which leads through my life into the world, and out of the world again."[1] This "line" consists of dreams, fantasies, hopes and desires, aimed at attaining some kind of relationship with the unconscious, as well as full participation and acknowledgment of the outer events that took place—good, bad, indifferent.

I believe the third requirement in psyche's education is the most difficult and challenging: to transcend the story itself, to grasp that one is not necessarily the victim of history, circumstance, and fate. To be "fully conscious to the end" is an exercise in the highest spiritual development.

I have realized that old age is the profoundest preparation for dying if it is lived fully, richly, determinedly, and hopefully in the vitality of the present moment. Each of us has a fantasy about "how I want to die." Terms like "gracefully," "suddenly," "painlessly," are often mentioned with the caveat that "I do not want a lingering illness, to die slowly." No one knows how death will come, but phrases like "not yet," "only when I've completed my life," and "not before I am ready," are common. I see now that only in the final interlude can one begin to appreciate the wisdom of Heraclitus: "We were born dying.

Joseph Wheelwright, the American Jungian analyst who lived well into his nineties, once remarked that the first task of old age was to withdraw projections from the world. I agree. The tragedy of old age is when projections are not withdrawn. This is the reason for the bitterness, disappointment, despair, anger, and brittleness regarding the world, as one realizes ever more fully that the world will never live up to one's projections. I know now that withdrawing projections is a lifelong work, and is never completed.

I have taken a keen interest in how individuals in the final interlude relate to their "end time." What follows are verbal photographs, portraits as it were, of individuals who have told their stories to me. Some presently live in assisted-care facilities; others live in their homes, and several have passed from the final interlude into the cloud of memory. As each faced the future in the final interlude of their life, their states of being were shared with me and for this I am grateful.

ADAM

In his ninety-seventh year

At ninety-seven, Adam still ponders the significant turning points of his life, the first being the death of his mother when he was thirteen. His grief only became real when he was older, but he recalls vividly that warmth and religion died when his mother died. He observes that he was never an "acceptor" but a "thinker." Acceptance was necessary only when he could not change a situation through thinking.

Adam was an avid tennis player until he was ninety. As he mused, he said that "love is exciting, but sex is boring." He does not have regrets about some path not chosen. He welcomes each day with a sense of wonder and has "an awe towards life." No one in his family wants to talk about death with him. He is clear though that he wants to die in the daytime and "wants to be conscious of what is happening" at the end.

When asked what advice he would give to those younger, he replied, "Don't be selfish, but be self-centered. View the world. Look at humming birds. Read two books: *The Prince and the Pauper* and *Robinson Crusoe*. Attitude is everything. Make each day count!"

His philosophy is simple: "I want to be self-fulfilling, yet I know it's not been a selfish life. If I were to go back, I'd teach a course on emotions. I'd instill a feeling for living. At ninety-seven, I'm fine by myself. At this stage of the game, who is it I have to impress?"

His family thought Adam demented and had been waiting for him to die, which he did, quietly in the morning hours at peace in his own home as he wanted.

MELANIE

In her ninety-second year

A vital and imaginative woman, Melanie is a retired psychological professional, and, after ten years of widowhood, at ninety-two she has found a new friend with whom to share life. Articulate and dynamic, she has dictated her thoughts regarding "the final interlude."

"As we begin to wind up our lives on this earth, the main task before us is actually the same one we have had at each transition: *to find our inner companion*. Until we know this inner friend, we continue to struggle. Often we hear of the need for the aging to 'tell their stories' because it is necessary to review a life as we come to the end. We need to know that, whatever happens to us, we must claim it as part of ourselves. We have to face our cruelty, our insensitivity, our stupidity, our deceitfulness, and our blindness without being crushed. Over and over again, older people tell me, 'I want to know who I am,' or 'I yearn to be alone, I want to find a quiet still place and be allowed to be there without interruption.' During all of the transitions of life, death has been present. We are constantly dying to an image we have of ourselves, to allow a new image to emerge. As we grow older, the images of death and rebirth seem to be shown to us more clearly."

Melanie has recently experienced great pain and suffering from accidental falls. Pain has been a reckoning force in the journey through the final interlude. Despite the pain, her lucidity prevails.

KARL
In his eighty-fifth year

Karl was abandoned at birth, a trauma that occupied years and years of analysis. His adoptive parents were loving, compassionate, and gave him and their adopted daughter an environment for growth and achievement. But in Karl's case, rather stern admonitions on sexuality, its explorations, and, to be sure the worst expressions of it with other boys formed the atmosphere of his growing years.

Later in the service of his country during World War II, he experienced compassionate and loving friendships, discovered canoeing, and expressed his masculinity very differently from that approved by his adoptive parents. He used the government's G.I. Bill of Rights to finance an educational journey that eventually ended with a doctorate in astronomy.

Emotionally unable to marry his college sweetheart, he married and remained in the marriage until the death of his wife. Fathering a son and daughter brought to him the public recognition of "normality." He joined a men's organization that healed his needs for masculine attention and persisted in the "kiva of friends" well into his eighties. However, *origins* persisted as he entered "the final

interlude" and after entering a retirement home, a
remarkable and life-changing event occurred—he
found his family of birth origin through the efforts
of a counselor in the retirement home. Suddenly, his
life was complete. His newly found twin brothers,
themselves in their late sixties, bonded with an older
brother they never knew they had. Yet, for Karl, the
discovery of the DNA connection to his birth father
has changed his sense of destiny. It appears that
his father was an excellent pianist who had perfect
pitch. Amazingly, Karl has both as well. To discover
a father at this time, and in addition to share in the
qualities with a father that Karl himself thought to
be singularly his has enriched the minutes, hours,
and days in Karl's final interlude. "Astonishing"
is too limiting a word for Karl. He has now two
fathers and mothers and cherishes all four.

Despite various and serious physical problems in
his early eighties, Karl is no longer besieged by a
haunting regarding origins. Pain became tolerable,
surgeries endurable as his life became a matter of
historical record with names, dates, place of origin,
and the lives of his true mother and father. At the
remarkable moment when he received actual photographs of parents and brothers, he felt he could die a
very happy man!

His life is filled with physiological agonies, including a gradual deterioration of sight. But his
inner sight is abundant, his daily habits of walking,

sharing, reading, and solving his favorite puzzles fill his life in "the final interlude" with joyousness and contentment. His son attends to his needs, his daughter writes regularly, and his brothers call weekly. His autobiography is now complete and the healing powers of his dreams comfort him, as the following dream sequence illustrates. *He realizes that he wants to reconcile with the two most import-ant women in his life—his deceased wife and an early romance before he married.* The dream feeling was intense and urgent. During his analytical hour, he sensed this urgency and experienced an astonishing relief from long pent-up silence. In a subsequent dream, *he is giving an astronomy lecture complete with slides. An astronomer listener is so helpful to the dreamer that he felt uplifted. The topic was of a giant red star as it uses up its last vitality, shedding the past as it turns off and disappears into the galaxy.* Karl's last statement regarding the dream was, "At last I am prepared to disappear into the galaxy." An eloquent and profoundly meaningful *postlude* for a life-cycle completed!

Margery
The woman who astounded

Margery died peacefully at ninety-six after a nine-teen-year struggle with breast cancer. She astounded medical professionals, as well as her family, friends, and acquaintances, with her vitality for life. No one believed her true age was ninety-six. She was so proud of her advanced age that she would amplify it by stating she "…was in her ninety-seventh year." Her commitment was to life.

Her commitment to life began early. She completed studies in social work and began her career as a psychiatric social worker in the notorious Hell's Kitchen neighborhood in Manhattan. Educating young children was her real passion and she did so throughout her life, founding schools for the young, including one in her hometown. What particularly interested her was in understanding how young children think. Her genius was in encouraging students to express themselves artistically. She retired from teaching at the age of eighty-two. Her activities continued by taking up yoga in her nineties, astounding fellow students half her age with her flexibility, a flexibility that was mental as well as physical.

In spite of her body slowing down, she remained sharp and bright, delighting in the presence of her grandchildren, and, when, regrettably, she could no longer speak, her family sang to her, read poetry to her. She revealed she heard it all with a little half-smile.

It was Margery's remarkable extroversion that sustained her—the vitality of the otherness in life, the joy of celebrating to her death the delight in *homo festivus* as well as *homo ludens*—to celebrate and to be filled with the creative spirit of play.

Dorothy

In her eighty-seventh year

Dorothy often describes her life as one that has "walked the yellow brick road." This statement has a poignancy because like Dorothy in *The Wizard of Oz*, she lived her life in search of wisdom figures, and in later life discovering her "wizards" in the founders of psychoanalysis and several gurus who led her into meditation practices.

Dorothy lives in a retirement center, and though in failing physical health, her psychical vitality and its expressions are nourishing to her many professional and personal friends. At eighty-seven, she reflects upon her journeys into church-related activities, family therapies, her journey to India and Tibet in search of solace and meditative possibilities of the East.

In a conversation, she asked if I found meditation as helpful in the final years of life as she had. To travel to the realms of peace and contentment has brought psychical energies that compensate for the frailty of the flesh. And through meditation, she lives in realms of awesome beauty. To experience the release from the body and its pain for the psychological and healing realms of meditation has brought Dorothy into the wisdom of her own being needing wizards no longer! She was able to reveal to her aging neighbor women her lifelong secret about herself. She declared to them after they had shared early male friendships: "Well, I think you ought to know that I am a lesbian." After a moments silence, the women with tears in their eyes, embraced Dorothy. It was the psychological courage in Dorothy's revelation that brought peace, safety, and security into her life.

In a fateful accident, she fell and broke her femur. The women mentioned above came to her rescue and negotiated the possibility of surgery, or, the longer term process of healing. Dorothy chose the latter, and, is grateful for her choice considering the trauma of a surgical procedure. She is spending her days in meditation and self-care.

It is fascinating to contrast Dorothy's reveries in the final interlude with the remarkable physical energies of Margery's life while living well into her nineties.

Observations

The case of Margery is in contrast to other moving examples of living in the final interlude. Margery lived in life's outer energies until her death. In contrast, Dorothy is living an introverted and nourishing life of meditation. When medical issues do not give the individual freedom of choice, and inner life is the greater totality in the final interlude, caretakers *must* have the wisdom to nurture it, allow it, and assist its presence.

What must be noted as critical and all-pervasive in the final interlude is the raging presence of waring contrasts. "Should I do this or that?" This is reminiscent of Hamlet's famous quandary: "To be or not to be; that is the question."

For those living in the final interlude, these Hamletics are posed daily.

Should I move to a retirement center or remain at home? Should I downsize now or wait until another day? Should I live alone or invite someone to share my home? Should I have a medical examination for the memory losses I experience now or later? Should I continue driving my automobile or take public transportation? Should I visit a senior center for company or remain content at home alone? Do I have the strength to travel by air, rail, or bus or remain dissatisfied at home? Should I consult a doctor about my need to nap or just continue doing it? Should I prepare my own meals or use frozen prepared meals? Should I consult a spiritual advisor or continue pondering on my own? Shall I bother my children with my life or keep my concerns to myself? Is there any way to rid myself of guilt over mistakes in the past or simply ignore them? Do I need to have a computer or is a telephone sufficient?

And so it goes. The questions that arise in the final interlude are so many and fill up one's daily life because these questions create discomforts, worries, concerns, bewilderments, alienations, aloneness, and other such plagues. It's the perpetual tension of decision-making that haunts and perturbs. To seek only personal answers and resist solutions others offer creates tensions in family and friendships, and, worse, to have solutions imposed by outside authorities negates any sense of personhood.

Regardless of education or background, each and every one of us becomes tormented and bewildered by this-or-that posing of questions. One must acknowledge that all is not well. Outer silence subsumes our lives, but the inner voices do not remain silent. Having a listener, and an empathetic and compassionate one, is not a luxury, but a necessity for mental and physical well-being. The difference in being talked *at* in contrast to being listened *to* needs no elucidation. It becomes the *sine qua non* of facilitation, nursing, counseling, and care. Respect for aging, the issues of aging, and the complexity of aging become critical in the final interlude.

The Indeterminate

There is one haunting and persistent question that those living in the final interlude ask. After many hours of counseling and reflecting, the inevitable return to the question dominates. The question is,

"What is my future?"

The "future" has been part of the life quest since childhood, early adulthood, and various attempts to consolidate the ego in relationship, family, career, and social consciousness to mention only the obvious. I am familiar with the case of a male professional who is now in the final interlude. His vexatious and persistent wondering "What I am going to be doing for the rest of my life" never abates. For him, "doing something" *is* living. "Having nothing to do" is a living purgatory. Advising, traveling, volunteering, coaching, consulting, or any activity imaginable is better than facing the ineluctable reality of life itself: *The future is, ultimately, dying and death.*

A life of "doing something" is what is hoped for; a life in the final interlude removes "doing something" for passing time, waiting, and vital living seems remote. Reckoning with this dilemma brings to mind a poem by the American poet of last century, Adelaide Crapsey, entitled *Triad* [2]:

> These be
> three silent things:
> The falling snow…the hour
> Before dawn…the mouth of one
> Just dead.

In her remarkable diction, the future is "silence" and the extreme opposite of the perpetual questions, meanderings, and the fraught mind. Pondering alternatives is a natural function of consciousness, but making a move in a direction requires courage, fortitude, and a resolute determination to explore as much as is possible.

Poised to intervene are the physical and mental health issues so prevalent in the final interlude. Choosing for oneself or having choices made by others, confronting limitations courageously, and living a life of satisfaction doing what one can— these are the dictates of the final interlude.

The Wonders of Aging in the Syntonic[3]

Living a satisfying life in the final interlude places emphasis upon the consciousness of those caretaking the aging to direct and permit the aging one to engage in self-realization and to overcome the continuing dictates of those nursing and caretaking. There is in our intellectual history a series of phrases that call attention to what one *can* do and can be *permitted* to do to enjoy a creative and surprisingly rich inner life. Discovering the exact word which names the task for those living in their eighties, nineties, and even into the hundreds can be a discovery and revelation. The word is *opsimath;* it means "learning late in life." Imagine hearing an aging one uttering, "I am an opsimath! I love learning late in life." And for purposes of ease, the small phrases that can assist in eliminating the *dystonic* (the discordant) in favor of the *syntonic* (the congenial and happy harmony in living) will be familiar to many in their Latin form:

> *Homo sapiens*
> *Homo faber*
> *Homo ludens*
> *Homo festivus*

Or, in English, "human knowing," "human doing and working," "human playing and creating," and "human celebrating and enjoying festivity." It is in these activities that one is the sole knower, maker, creator in words and images, and, lastly, the celebrant, and the discoverer of the distinctive personal expressions that are *not* dictated by others, but are discovered within oneself. Imagine the joy in discovering within oneself, "the self-declared opsimath!"[4]

To live in the syntonic, particularly in the final interlude, is to experience a freedom of choice in life's changing moments whether living freely or being cared for by others. In the dystonic, what others require, desire, organize in a time frame, while attending to the myriad issues with the physical body, and "keeping to the rules of an institution," sacrifices human choice. True, serious illnesses impede living in the 80s, 90s, and 100s, and become what is so obvious—a breathing, compliant patient, unable to satisfy their own desires. So, assuming well-being and a vital consciousness, the individual awaits the pleasures of the syntonic.

The one who strives to know is being a learner, eager to "learn about" every aspect of what is happening in the interior body, but also eager to "learn about" what is happening in a world that is no longer within the learner's grasp. The one who strives to know is "learning to be" and in the process experiencing a "sense of becoming." This is celebrated by sensing and knowing contexts rather than an emphasis on content. Contexts reveal where I am, what is happening, and is an inner compass orienting the aging person to the rapid changes occurring in the world of the 21st century.

The person who is a maker and also is striving to create, lives in a syntonic world and participates in understanding the "map" created of the world and the world beyond. The result is centered on *knowing* and *becoming*, and, should it be required, becoming one with a world newly defined. The effect is to reframe the world from the impinging and the destructive to one where the knower experiences an incredible sense of interconnection and new learning.

The person who can play is free to make, to express in word, music, image or other forms of expression. And what is revealed is who the person is. The reader will recall that the Latin for man as a player is *homo ludens.*[5]

In a curious historical accident, the most obvious English word with "play" in it is "ludicrous." Nothing could be more devaluing of "play" than "ludicrous," a dystonic linguistic remnant. No, play is inherently not ludicrous. Play is a releasing and exploring moment in whatever the "play" may be— writing, singing, dancing, playing a game, an athletic moment, working artistically. It is sad, but true, that to be in the spirit of play and its limitless reaches is gravely overlooked in education and care of the aged. It would not surprise anyone to realize that "education" means a "knowing human" (*Homo sapiens*), while exploring play and its incredible possibilities (*Homo ludens*) is seen as a luxury and denied.

It is in the creative balance and interaction of knowing, playing, and working (*homo faber*), that the human condition becomes alive and vital to the context in which it lives, and the context becomes more critical than just learning content. Merely meditate upon how the word "work" dominates our lives and its absence in the final interlude is not only missed but is detrimental.

Playing is the matrix of all art forms: music, poetry, painting, sculpture, as well as idiosyncratic playful forms of the maker's invention. Consider that cell phones now offer a motion picture possibility of documenting life's evanescence and therefore possibilities of play.

Within this amazingly rich syntonic world of selection, choices, creation, play, life in the final interlude allows for individual expression, expression poignant and personal. Allowing the mind's effortless activities, the sense of working things out, playing with all manner of expressions, and finding celebrations possible from the past, present, and into the future, releases one to ponder, to admire, and to share.[6]

The suggestion is made that wise people ". . . try to understand situations from multiple perspectives, not just their own, and they show tolerance as a result."[7] Syntonic living in the final interlude allows aging to be viewed from perspectives of a mind, a mind discovering its own sense of wisdom through a generativity that ". . . gives back without needing anything in return."[8] This creative process helps to ward off the dystonic despairs of depression, a sense of being lost, of living up to the expectations of others, or essentially losing a sense of being an *individual*, a word meaning "incapable of being divided." In a telephone conversation with a woman whose husband now in his nineties is slowly ebbing with a chronic disease, I asked about him and she replied that it was only a matter of time before he passed, but, she added, at the moment he is playing the piano. I loudly exclaimed, "Wonderful! It is the most psychologically healing thing he could do at the moment!" This is a brilliant example of how an individual can seek the syntonic and overcome the chronic dystonic.

Old age is not necessarily only decline; it also can rally inner mental forces to celebrate the inevitable movement towards death. The following poem was written by an eighty-five-year-old man, a retired professor, and one who lives as richly as possible in the syntonic.

Winter Words at Eighty-five

Words are less facile now
Weighted as they are by recollections.
In the summer and spring of life
Words were carelessly flung.
But now, words are wintry
And more akin to the intricacies
Of snowflakes
Than a summer's meadow.
Having outlived all family members,
I approach the Season of the Final Interlude
With a carol of my own. . .
Hark! Listen to the wind and rain
And recall, if you can, a world without pain,
A world that is innocent of warring stain.
Look! See the sunset's reddening glow
And ponder day's ending and know
The sameness of sunset's light and winter snow.

The Discovery of Epiphanies

The primary challenge of life in the final interlude is to remain mentally vital and creative in exploring the journeys of the mind and its mindfulness, its capacity to work at problems, its exploration of playfulness in image-making for the eye, the ear, and delight in story and poem. To experience the astonishing presence of a creation taking place from oneself is life's most sterling expression of the creative spirit. Researchers have found that with age "…people become biased in their memory toward words and associations that have a positive connotation—the age-related positivity effect as it is known."[9] Being encouraged to create, particularly in the final interlude, is an awakening in the aging mind even if the creations reflect on life's end.

In the end, we are told, the summary is complete. In that frail hovering between life and death, before our eyes passes a parade of images that succinctly and without commentary narrate the story of our life in the milliseconds to infinity's entrance. To have seen one's life in that moving scenario of images, to have sensed the best of life's pulse and moment does not have to wait for the end, but can be experienced in a variety of possibilities in vital waking moments of creative exploration. C.G. Jung himself enjoined this to old age when he wrote, "In old age one begins to let memories unroll before the mind's eye and, musing, to recognize oneself in the inner and outer images of the past. This is like a preparation for an existence in the hereafter."[10]

The final interlude can be characterized by a tension between deterioration of body and mind and the re-creation of mental energies that sustain and frame daily life. One man sustained his life by making music: *playing the piano*. For another, *the writing of a poem*. And for others, *drawing, sewing, singing, slow dancing*. In short, old age can be a dis-covery again of *Homo ludens, Homo festivus*, and by sheer meditation, exemplifying what we are, *Homo sapiens*. Dr. Marc. C. Agronin trenchantly observes that, "Old age…is less a product of nature and more of a human achievement wrestled from nature."[11] He continues: "In old age, we might affirm, may your presence still be meaningful to others. May you receive the care you need. May you still retain some strengths. May you benefit from mutual interac-tions."[12] Agronin's affirmations are nothing else but a plan for the syntonic possibility; the absence of his affirmations would certainly activate the dystonic.

The Need to Sense Home

Where the final interlude is being lived is crucial for having a sense of the syntonic. Without a sense of home, the situation is fraught with the potential for the dystonic. So real can be the fear in an aging person of being placed "in a home," that the individual feels a loss of control in life and living. After a placement in a retirement center, nursing home, or congenial institution, it is vital to make the room, single or shared, have important reminders of one's lived life: pictures, objects, remnants of a previous home, and the like.

Karl, while fiercely resistant to "moving into a home," finally did so. He created a "new home" in one room with the key objects, pictures, books, CDs of his favorite music, to mention only a portion of what the new "home" reflected of that "past home." Similarly, in the case of Dorothy, her women friends brought family photos, pictures of her guru, cards and notes sent to her from friends and former colleagues. And here Dorothy rests content with full view of artifacts of her past. Her past home is now a small wall of visual memories, sufficient in size and scope to make her life as syntonic as possible.

In the final interlude, home is a cascade of memories from the past some of which are visible on an opposite wall. The dystonic would be an institutionalization, a stark place, with naked walls, and a feeling of cell block, not of home. If possible, the individual would do whatever necessary to experience home comfort, but in the bereft state only the dystonic would prevail. How fortunate it is for those living in the final interlude to do so in comfort and contained either in the home, or a home that resonates with a past life's experiences.

Personal Cultural Facets and the Collective Cultural Life

In the final interlude, much depends upon the quality and availability of mindfulness that is responsive to life's past and present. To have a wall or a room filled with one's artifacts, pictures, and possessions is a substitute for the familiarity of a home and its longtime nurturing. However, there is also the collective cultural memories and facets important to a life, even if the memories of a cultural life harken to the past. In the final interlude, the current or present cultural life may not have any, or perhaps only a fragmentary conscious awareness of "the outside world." Those living in the final interlude should have the compassionate concern of care providers to allow "living in the past" in all forms. Compassion and empathy are the hallmarks of care, and the awakenings that occur with such care sustain life's personal as well as recalled cultural inner journey.

In the case of Karl, his skill as a pianist has persisted into his eighties. And the music he plays? The music of the 1930s and 40s. The facility in which he lives allows him to entertain all who live there with the music of their shared past. The emotional powers of singing "old-time" lyrics is a compassionate and empathic merging of present inner with former outer life. In contrast, Melanie loves to read and re-read the novels of her girlhood with little interest in anything contemporary. Her past cultural memories are tied to the books "that changed her life."

With the contemporary availability of films on DVD, those childhood and adolescent memories of Saturday matinées resonate in the psyches of those who can and do recall their youth. Such an event took place with the death of Mickey Rooney at ninety-three. After the age of forty, his artistic life halted, as it were, but his memory is captured by his own filmed boyhood and adolescence. His story is repeated over and over again by actors and actresses of his generation who continue to move those in their 90s and 100s. The past is life remembered; the present is a confusion of multiple elements; the future, of course, that which awaits and terminates life.

But, what if for any number of accountable reasons, an individual living in the final interlude asks for or requires psychological treatment? What would be appropriate?[13] Dr. Agronin cites four common therapeutic failures by care givers with those living in the final interlude: *Ignorance*—where there is a lack of knowledge and understanding of age-specific issues and diagnoses on the part of the care giver; *Confusion*—age-centricity by the care giver and an inability to have empathy for the life and times of the aging; *Prejudice*—care givers who have attitudes that denigrate the aging on the basis of age alone; and *Negation*—care givers who become pessimistic about improvement in the aging.[14] In short, those who facilitate and help those living in old age must be free of biases and prejudices and facilitate with compassion and empathy.

There are behavioral manifestations amongst the aging that both the aging person and caregiver can perceive, becoming alert to the inner processes to which they point. Consider the symptoms in the ninth stage: Depression, anxiety, mania, psychosis, obsessive-compulsive disorder, complaints of body pain without obvious signs of pain, genuine pain, and, confusion.

Despite all the possibilities for symptoms as suggested above, the therapeutic community that treats those in the final interlude have discovered that perhaps the most helpful therapeutic statement that can be given is a stunningly powerful and penetrating compassionate one. And that statement? Simply, *I believe in your ability to recover.* There is hope of nothing less than the ability to transcend the complexities of living in the final interlude.[15]

Making and Helping to Make the Transition to the Final Interlude

John Hill, in his remarkable book, *At Home in the*

World: Sounds and Symmetries of Belonging,[16] notes
that whatever the age, transitions are difficult. They
are the moments when all seems lost, empty, uncon-
tained. We are not created to remain in a void, yet in
those liminal moments fundamental questions arise
concerning the meaning of "home." As we move
through the stages of life, at the end we face ultimate questions. Do we belong anywhere, to anyone?
Is the graveyard our ultimate abode? Is our final
destiny simply to live on in the memories of others?
Do we have a home in another world beyond our
life on earth?[17]

It must be stressed that the sense of a home is
crucial to all living in the final interlude—in the
home of the individual with a caretaker at hand, a
retirement community with care facilities, a nursing
home with a single bed or double-bed room, whatever the arrangement, it matters profoundly that the
inner life of the individual be as syntonic as possible. A dystonic situation creates a sense of despair
and aloneness, and the inner life, where every single
individual lives, is slowly eroded into blankness. The
import of this is simple: every opportunity must be
taken to activate and fill the inner life. To repeat the
possibilities: being with others for conversations,
games, viewing films and television; sharing dining
room tables morning, noon, evening; if alone, enjoying reading, viewing films, television, solving jigsaw
puzzles, writing poems and short pieces; sharing

leisurely walks, or exercising lightly with others; sharing books and encouraging conversations about them; creating a sewing circle; perhaps an interest group—political, religious, or whatever appeals to two or more folk.

In short, living in the final interlude, if at all possible, is one of pursuing aspects of a creative life, a relational life, an entertaining life, a reading curiosity whether read personally or listened to from an audio-book, but most hopefully, a curious life that is still interested in the outer world as well as the inner world.

REFLECTIONS

Russell Lockhart

The Story of Bob

When I was younger, I was known as a Young Turk, always eager to take on challenges. Such it was that I told the nurses in a geriatric unit that I wanted to work with a patient who was unresponsive in their view, one who they might whisperingly call a "vegetable." No lack of vegetables, I was told, and was promptly connected with an 80-something-year-old man I will call "Bob." Bob spent his time in bed or wheelchair and stared far off into space as his primary activity. I began my project by wheeling him up to a table and I sat beside him. On the table were large sheets of newsprint and crayons in front of us both.

I began by placing a crayon in his hand. I took up a crayon and drew a line across my sheet. I took his hand and did the same on his sheet so he could have the sensation. This was repeated a number of times on that first day, and the next. On the third or fourth day, I began by drawing a circle on my sheet. I waited. I looked at Bob, looked into his eyes and down at his page. Nothing. His hand twitched. Nothing unusual as he had a slight tremor at all times. Still, I had patience.

A couple of days later, I drew my circle. To my surprise and delight, he began to draw one as well. Not a really round circle, but a tremulous circle. He was doing it! The next day, I did my circle and added a couple of dot-eyes. He did the same. I was beginning to get excited. I drew in a mouth. So did he. I patted him on the shoulder, gave him a big smile.

The next day, I drew the face, the eyes, a nose dot, a smiley mouth. I waited for him to follow and he did. Then, to my utter surprise, he drew in a pipe and then a curling line. Smoke! We looked at each other and his smile was something I can still see nearly a half-century later. The staff was dumbfounded when I showed them.

I began to wonder how far Bob and I could go with this. The next day, I did not draw, but Bob took up his crayon and drew the face and then the pipe. He put down the crayon. He did not draw the smoke. I looked at him, my puzzlement I'm sure was obvious. But Bob did not draw the smoke. The next day he began again and after drawing the face put down the crayon. He did not draw the pipe. As I looked into his eyes I could see tears forming.

When I came the next day, I did not find Bob in his usual place. I went to the nurses' station to inquire. The head nurse came out and met me. She put her hand on my shoulder and said, "Bob died last night."

I felt unsteady, a bit dizzy, and nauseous. I reached out and hugged the nurse until my reaction subsided and gave way to my own tears. As I left the unit and walked slowly back to my office, I began to focus on the pipe, the image Bob had produced spontaneously. Where did that come from? I decided to look at Bob's records. Since he had been there for a very long time, this was not so easy to do and involved going into storage and retrieving his files. I was able after considerable effort to find his admissions file. There, I discovered that when he was admitted, he had a pipe and it was taken from him.

Bob had been without his pipe for more than 30 years. Yet, even in his "vegetative" state, the memory was alive and he spontaneously produced its image and it was lit up, with smoke rising. And then, in a poignant denouément, the smoke goes out, the pipe disappears, and Bob dies.

The fact that "art" enabled access to this memory; the fact that the memory was still alive; the fact of spontaneous expression of psychic life unknown to the outside world; the synchrony of the disappearance of the smoke and the pipe and Bob's dying as if illustrating an intuition that his fire of life was going out. All this impressed that Young Turk I was then, impressed me of the intense valuation of *interiority*, the unseen psychic life in even the most unlikely places. This has served as a foundation for my work as an analyst for more than 40 years.

And what do I get from remembering this now, writing it now? Put simply, there are things I want to remember before I die, to connect up with again, to gather perhaps, not as a nostalgic defense against demise, but as a way of threading together the bits and pieces that I have been, that I have done, that I have seen, and felt and loved. Art will be a part of this because it has the potential for reaching deeper down, farther back, into the deepest depths of me.

The Power of the Small

Laurens van der Post is sitting across from me at the Miramar Hotel in Santa Monica, famous for its fabulous inhabitants over the years: Greta Garbo, Jean Harlow, Marilyn Monroe and an endless list of the rich and famous. I was lunching with the man who was not yet knighted, trying to get some bits and pieces to use in my introduction of him later that night. He's gone now, but my memory of our conversation remains sharp and sparkly like his eyes were that day back in the 70's somewhere.

At one point, I asked him, "What was the most important thing you learned when you were with the Bushmen?" Without a pause, he answered, "the power of the small." What he referred to was the keen observation of small things, often overlooked, unnoticed, while one's mind is occupied with big things. As example, he said that if he was fearful of a dangerous animal attacking him, if his mind filled up with that image, then he would not notice the movement of the little creeping, crawling things on the ground, the undulating grasses; he would not feel the subtle movements of air, the change in the background harmonies of sound. If your mind is too full of what you consciously fear you will miss the small things that have the power to save your life.

What van der Post told me that day left an indelible impression on me and came to be one of the principles on which I work with dreams and live my life. I'm not always up to remembering it, but something always occurs to give me another object lesson in the validity of what van der Post told me.

There is perhaps no bigger idea, no bigger reality as we get older and move into the final stages of life, into the final interlude, than death. Still, as I approach death, however close or far off it may be, I want to work toward remembering what I learned: to focus on the "small." If our mind is too full of fear, too full of pain, too full of regret, too full of yearning for the beyond, too full of most anything, then we are likely to miss the most crucial of things: small, unnoticed, unattended, but inhabiting our diminishing world nonetheless, waiting, wondering, if our notice will come.

Eggs

Eggs. My earliest memory. In the old Buick, in the back seat, window rolled down, I was nearly three. My parents had brought some grocery bags and put them in the back seat and went back for more. In those days, it was OK to leave your kid for a moment by himself in the car. I discovered a carton of eggs. I remember taking them one by one and dropping them out the window and leaning over watching them break open. What fun that was! I remember too my parents happening upon this scene, my father pointing, and breaking out in laughter, while my mom followed suit. My childhood was full of laughing times like this. Makes it difficult to hear the tales of abuse I have heard during all my years as an analyst. Makes me want to finish that essay, which a dream had titled, "The Importance of Being Silly," in honor of my father—perhaps his greatest gift to me.

So why focus on such a young memory when I'm writing on aging?

One's earliest memory often forms a *leitmotif* that becomes a major thread running through one's life uniting in some odd way many experiences. Here for example, I connect my science fair project on the anatomy of the chicken egg, and I recall the delight in telling people that the inner and outer membranes between the shell and the egg white were made from the protein keratin, the same protein as in human hair and nails. I was called an egg-head most of my life and I suppose I was and still am. Then there was the dream voice that announced: *Do you not know that words are eggs, that words carry life, that words give birth?* Working with that dream became first a lecture, then an article, then a book, long out of print, and now will cost you a pretty penny to obtain an original copy. But it has not set well with me to have this book out of print, so I have recently had it reprinted—a new egg, if you will.[18] I could mention many other egg things on this thread, but this is enough to make my point.

What does this have to do with aging? *Single* memories alone become easily fragmented, broken, and forgotten, particularly under the ravages of the myriad dementias to which aging invariably subjects us in varying degrees. But I have found in my work with aging people older than me, as well as myself, and those who begin to suffer the loss of memory, that *threads* of memory are held onto and held together much longer and better and continue to serve as themes to which one can add new experiences like beads on a thread. I have seen dreams do this, both in terms of bringing to the fore again an older memory as well as a new image, a pearl belonging on that leitmotif thread of memory.

Love & Neurogenesis

Perhaps it's not how long one lives, but how well one loves. For all the focus on health, staying fit, aging well, delaying the onset of dementia, and all the rest, there is very little emphasis on how to inhabit the geographies of love ever more fully as the years roll on. The geographies of love are endless, but as we age, it is all too frequent that we focus on loves lost, opportunities missed, possibilities thrown away, and fall victim to the tormenting bitterness that inevitably follows. Bitterness ages us more quickly than most anything else, and we would do well to find ways around the thickets that bitterness puts in our way. To love oneself more fully, to love others more fully, to love life itself more fully, to find new loves in new ways, in new places, these things undoubtedly will excite the neurogenesis of even the aging brain, brighten one's spirit, and awaken the soul to its coming encounter.

Upon Remembering My Mother's B12 Shots

During one summer as a teenager, I worked in downtown Los Angeles as a courier for Bank of America. I would have lunch at a Clifton's Cafeteria. It was an "oldsters" place as we called it then, full of elderly people and not really a place for high-hormone teens, but it was close and quick. Sitting there, one could overhear conversations because the oldsters spoke loudly—being hard of hearing and all. What I heard were stories of who had died, who was in hospital, who had suffered this and that. We thought of it as something of a medical horror show and vowed we'd never be like that.

In my 76th year now, in the middle of my eighth decade, I'm hard of hearing. Friends, relatives, and acquaintances are dead and dying. I've spent my time in hospital, with this surgery and that. Visits to the doctor are more frequent and of varying kinds. Treatments, pills, warnings. I'm one of those oldsters now.

Mortality shadows every move, glimpsed around every corner. I still don't want to be an oldster shouting out the latest medical bulletin or running down the score card of who's left. Nonetheless, something *compels* talking about these things—just like those people did way back when I was a teenager. What is this? Certainly the body is foregrounded, but I feel the mystery of it is much deeper.

I've been experiencing a return of a set of symptoms that first appeared after having open heart surgery 14 years ago. *Ataxia*, it's called—lack of coordination—ICD 781.3 (oh, yes, those numbers are part of the mystique of aging, making it all so *orderly*). My typing deteriorates. I veer to the left when walking. I bump into things. So, I return to my neurologist, who had treated me the last time this occurred with high levels of B12 supplements. Even mild B12 deficiency can produce such symptoms. Even no deficiency at all can produce symptoms if the problem is with the *absorption* of B12. My symptoms did disappear with the supplements.

But now they are back.

I'm being examined again. Additional symptom this time. I'm losing surface skin sensitivity in my lower legs. Also possible with B12 deficiency. In researching B12 deficiency, I discover it is underdiagnosed in the older population, with perhaps 40-50% of those over 60 afflicted. This is unrecognized in general medical practice. Symptoms of aging are seen as the cause of a wide variety of complaints, when many of these symptoms can be mimicked and masked by B12 deficiency and B12 absorption issues.

The neurologist once again orders the blood tests and says the likely treatment will increase the B12 supplementation, perhaps this time with B12 shots. At this mention of shots, I am stunned speechless in the face of a stream of powerful memories filling my experience: one image after another of my mother talking about her B12 shots. I realize that even though taking B12 *pills,* I had not once remembered B12 *shots.* I see my mother, lying on the couch looking quite cheery at the prospect of an imminent visit by Dr. Dixon to give her the shot. Yes, in those days doctors "rounds" often included stopping off to give shots, administer little treatments in patient's homes before going home for the day.

This memory came unbidden, and I found myself reflecting on the difference between unbidden memories and memories that are consciously searched for. As an oldster, I'm well aware of the frequent fruitlessness of *fishing* for a memory—a person's name, the quality of some place, the character in a book, a date. I'm aware too of the sensual pleasure one can experience when a memory comes unbidden, returns of its own accord, visits without invitation.

Mnemosyne comes right in without knocking. The goddess of memory and the mother of the Muses I welcome to my reflections and immediately I have a thought: what would oldsters do if they submitted their unbidden memories (you know, all those *old memories* that persist even when short-term memory begins to wane), not just *repeating* them (which so aggravates others), but putting them into active relationship with one of the nine muses?

On the next page there is a table of the nine muses, their names, their domain, and their primary emblems courtesy of Wikipedia—which, along with Google, is a kind of oldster's trunk of things forgotten and recallable now so readily on the computer—something akin to an external brain.

Muse	Domain	Emblem
Calliope	Epic poetry	Writing tablet
Clio	History	Scrolls
Euterpe	Music, Song, and Elegiac Poetry	Aulos (an ancient Greek musical instrument like a flute)
Erato	Lyric poetry	Cithara (an ancient Greek musical instrument in the lyre family)
Melpomene	Tragedy	Tragic mask
Polyhymnia	Hymns	Veil
Terpsichore	Dance	Lyre
Thalia	Comedy	Comic mask
Urania	Astronomy	Globe and compass

In my experience, oldsters (including myself) tend to repeat memories (sometimes *ad nauseum*). This is the primary characteristic of a *habit* and habits tend to be a double-edged sword for the aging brain. Of course, habits conserve energy and make efficient use in relation to things needing doing in repeating ways. But habits do not induce or facilitate *neurogenesis*, that is, the growth of *new* brain cells—yes, even in the aging brain—so necessary to remaining vital, healthy, and warding off the dementias of the later years.

So I have this clear memory of my mother awaiting her B12 shot. Looking at the list of muses and their realms, I can see that one way of working with this memory is to put it into a poem under the guidance of Calliope. Or, following Clio's lead, I could research the history of this B12 problem in my family. Erato would challenge me to write a love poem in relation to remembering my mother's B12 shots. Euterpe would have me write a song and sing it. Is there a song about Vitamin B12 shots? I know of none. Melpomene and her tragic mask would lead me into writing the tragic aspects of what lies behind the need for B12 shots. Polyhymnia wants a hymn to B12 shots. Terpsichore wants me to dance a dance of B12 shots. Thalia wants some comedy, perhaps some B12 jokes. And Urania wants me to look at the sky with B12 shots in mind and see what I see there.

Looked at this way, any unbidden memory returning to consciousness becomes an invitation from the muses to *create* something from this memory. Notice that none of the muses has anything to do with *meaning*. Hence, we are not looking for the meaning of the memory (which more than likely would keep us only embedded in the past), but for the memory to become the prompt, the inducement, for creative expression in some form. I suspect our thirst for meaning would be slated more productively following this hint than in the direct pursuit of meaning.

What then of those memories that we do go seeking after, trying to recall, trying to recover something of what we have forgotten: a dream, a person's name, a relative's birthday, whatever it might be. What then?

Of course, if we remember, we could follow the muse path as described above. However, since there is no guarantee that we can be successful in actively recovering the memory, we cannot call upon the muses until it returns, at some future time.

I think pursued memories put us in a different geography than those memories that return unbidden. What returns unbidden as I type these words is the old Norse god *Mimir* who lives in the roots of the Yggdrasil ("World Tree") guarding the well of wisdom. No muses here. There is a sense of danger. I recall Odin sacrificing his eye for the secret from the well. Yet, from his sacrifice he was rewarded with knowledge, knowledge of the runes. Digging into the roots of the word *Mimir*, we find the etymological root (s)mer-, literally meaning "to remember." Our word "mourn" comes from this root, as do the words "memory," "memorable," "memorandum," "commemorate," "remember." In Latin, it produced the word *memor*, meaning "to be mindful."

Thus, forgetting, and not being able to recall, puts us in mind of *trying* to remember. As one grows older, this becomes more of an effort, a struggle, painful, embarrassing. The roots tell us there is something to *mourn* here. How does one mourn the forgotten memory? We do not do this, we must have the memory back, or something is wrong. But what? I think it is because we are reminded of our mortality. Forgotten memories are preparations for our own being forgotten. Memories die, just as we do, and *before*.

Is there a *risk* in trying to recall, to remember, to make all this effort?

The other day, someone I was working with, was struggling with trying to recall the year in which a certain event occurred. She was becoming more and more frustrated at her inability to remember. I interrupted her efforts then, and without telling her why, lit a candle and asked her to hold it and look into the flame and empty her mind as fully as possible. Just watch the flame. After a short time, tears began to streak down her cheeks. She let them flow, didn't even reach for a tissue After a while, she straightened up, blew out the candle and said, "Thank you."

Without my having to ask, she described how the memory of seeing her father in his casket at his funeral presented itself to her and when this happened she began to cry, something she could not do at her father's funeral. It was the year of her father's death she had been trying to remember, and now she knew the date, but remembering the date itself was not nearly as important as the experience she had in relation to the unbidden memory and the tears that flowed from its arrival.

This suggests to me that ego grasping after a forgotten memory, stands in the way of something more important than just remembering, and that is opening oneself to what psyche spontaneously presents, presents unbidden. Once this happens, we are again in the precincts of the muses and can now use ego energies to manifest the creative possibilities of the presentational psyche.

What Does Death Want?

I was with my daughter Sharon when she died. I saw her take her last breath. I saw the heart monitor level out and flat line. I leaned down and kissed her forehead and whispered, "Goodbye, girl." She died as she wanted to die. Afterwards, I was seized

by a question: *What does death want?* As I left to
"make arrangements," I walked and walked and this
question was like a buzzing hive of bees in my head.
"Babbles the bee in a stolid ear." Emily Dickenson's
line came unbidden to mind. And then this:

> *The flesh surrendered, cancelled,*
> *The bodiless begun;*
> *Two worlds, like audiences, disperse*
> *And leave the soul alone.*[19]

Does death leave the soul alone? Was this Dickenson's projection of her sequestered life on what
comes after, or was this a deeper insight? I'd often
said that though everyone dies, our death is our
most individual experience, and one in which we
are absolutely alone. Could that "singularity" hold
true beyond? Odd thoughts after breathing in my
daughter's final exhalation, her death.

That night, after some difficulty getting to sleep, I
was visited by this dream.

> *I see a "building." This is where Sharon is.*
> *The outside of the building is a flux of colors*
> *and flowers of all kinds, swirling, swirling.*
> *There is no way into or out of this building.*
> *But watching the flow and flux of color and*
> *flowers is extraordinary and generates a peace*
> *that is deep and profound. It is as if the building*
> *itself is alive--but not even as if; it is alive.*

In the morning, when writing down the dream, I felt blessed by it. Still under the sway of Dickenson's poetry, I wrote some lines in the margin of the dream:

> *How excellent the dying*
> *When arrival's come to this:*
> *A building of flowers alive*
> *Happy, she's with the swirling*

I can't imagine too many people would take to the idea of the "soul alone" as what comes after death, as what death wants. Dickenson, yes. And, I must admit, I find the idea itself alluring. I've no religious belief to stand in the way of pursuing this image to whatever ends it will lead me. But leading me it is, and I will follow and what comes of that will be my final answer to what death does want.

LEE & RUSS IN CONVERSATION

Russ. Let's talk about the way dreams might be used in relation to aging. For example, I have worked with quite a few people who are in their "final interlude." With all of these people, in looking at their dreams, I have yet to see a dream that focuses specifically on aging.

Lee. I would agree.

Russ. I'm wondering what your experience has been in working with people who are in this stage.

Lee. I've had individuals dream of aged persons: grandmothers, grandfathers, aged teachers. But the dreaming of aging itself: I haven't seen it and you haven't seen it. We need to reflect on this.

Russ. I think it may relate as well to Jung's observation and von Franz' observation that when it comes to death itself, dreams seem to ignore the issue. In spite of how much focus there might be from a conscious point of view or a conscious perspective on one's dying, when it comes to the dreams themselves, the focus is always on some futurity, some future thing, images that have futurity in them. They don't seem to be talking about an end. My orientation to dreams emphasizes their future orientation *at all times*. I find that dreams are by their very nature more pointed toward the future than to the past. Yet most of the way that we work with dreams orients them and the work with them towards the past. We try to understand in terms of things already understood. Or, we try to formulate or reformulate some sense of the past that will make sense of the dream in the present. All that misses the futurity that is part of the very nature of dreaming. To me, a person approaching death with dreams not responding with images of endings, or stoppings, but with a sense of ongoingness of some kind, suggests that the ability to focus on dreams for people that are in their advancing years would be a fruitful source of vitality and futurity. This futurity of the dream argues against this looking back, fearing an end, and that sense of everything stopping, no hope, no future. The dreams themselves argue against this. So it seems to me that the dream is a rich resource for people growing older, a way to connect with something that is vital in their own process, something they cannot get from the collective, or from family or friends or others because everybody is so focused on "the end." The idea of some futurity has little foothold in this atmosphere.

Lee. The only manifestation I've experienced has been with those folks who have joined the Neptune

Society. I joined the Neptune Society years ago in Chicago and I'm still a member of the Neptune Society. Somehow that decision, as simple as it was to make, does not have the resonance of the kind you are exploring. I've taken care of the end and I will be taken out to sea. I am certain I have never dreamt of anything related to the Neptune Society, but I have worked with individuals who have made that decision to deal with the processes to occur upon death. Have you done that?

Russ. We have that provision in our wills. Not the Neptune Society, but similar group in Marysville, where we had Sharon cremated and so would use them as long as we are here in this area.

Lee. Where were Sharon's ashes put?

Russ. In Central Park in New York. That was her favorite place. When she explored New York she really liked the high energy there. Her high energy was at home in New York. So that's where she is.

Lee. If we make plans regarding our death what is there to dream of unless you're a passionate fundamentalist?

Russ. It is intriguing to me that dreams themselves do not focus on death or dying. They focus on images that have a quality of "the future." Early on in the development of humans this quality may have become a source for the sense of afterlife and this became elaborated into the mythologies and religions of "afterlife" that we are all familiar with.

When we became human, dreams probably had a much more profound effect on how people actually lived and how they related to things then is true now. Who pays attention to dreams now? In terms of some percentage of the collective population of 7 billion people in the world how many are paying attention to their dreams? As an evolutionary process dreams have probably fallen by the wayside. But early on, if they had the same qualities of futurity as they do now, this must have given people a sense of ongoingness of some kind.

Lee. Dreams do help in the unfolding of life through the stages of life. Even in the final interlude of one's 80's and 90's, it may be that dreams are an ongoing source of the energy of transition. If dreaming takes place into old age, into the final interlude, there is an energy there that is "not death."

Russ. One of the things we want to point out and make clear is how useful paying attention to one's dreams can be in the later years. I have seen people who are in their final interlude and they exhibit the usual characteristics of depression and collapse. The common pattern is to be more and more focused on health. In extremes, everything talked about has to do with the condition of the body, as if the body becomes a kind of magnetic or gravitational core that pulls conscious energy toward it. One can spend the whole day dealing with the body. Yet, I have seen in these situations, a dream will break through the fog of all that body focus and change the person's consciousness entirely.

Lee. I had a dream of my father. (He died many years ago. He was the victim of a hit-and-run driver. He had a terrible recovery, but passed away rather peacefully.) I was introducing him to a group of people, but it wasn't the physical image of my father. It was another man entirely! I've been intrigued by that. That's the closest I have come in terms of the "living image" of one who has died. He was alive and vital in this dream.

Russ. Well the dream itself is very alive. It has that potential like dreams that can occur during this period, of being very enlivening. If one focuses on this one can get nourished and enlivened by that dream. Now that takes the focus off the body and into a realm that is psychic and has this kind of future quality. Future quality partly because your father has died yet he's alive in the dream. Your father is not the specific physical image you knew, but is now different, an energy of some kind that is now your psychic father. So your psychic father is different than your actual father. *Something* is making the point that you are not introducing your actual father to the audience. And as audience we can't help but think of the audience for our writing. So you are introducing your psychic father to the audience that we are talking to.

Lee. You are making the point that we don't

dream about death and dying. Speaking for myself, I dreamed of an energy in my life that I wanted to introduce. Now if that's psyche in the final interlude *recapitulating* life's energies, that is something very different than death and dying.

Russ. Absolutely!

Lee. Jung observed, "Thoroughly unprepared we take this step into the afternoon of life. We take this step with the false assumption that our truths and ideals will serve us as hitherto. But we cannot live the afternoon of life according to the program of life's morning. For what was great in the morning will be little at evening. And what in the morning was true will at evening become a lie."[20]

Russ. How necessary it seems as we get older and older, and in particular as we get into the final interlude, that we must not be content with focusing only on what we've lost. This occupies so much of older people's consciousness. So much focus on loss: losing body functions, losing friends, losing partners, losing everything. But if one continues to dream, something essential is not lost.

Lee. One loses the capacity for decisions easily made earlier. So, as life becomes more dystonic, the problem is how to celebrate the syntonic through the *mind*. One way, certainly, is through dreams. How little this is recognized!

Russ. This has to do with what is gained by entering the final interlude. In so many other cultures the elderly are honored because they have entered into something that the younger people cannot know yet. But in our culture, our American culture, all of this is cut off because after we are 65, we are no longer young, no longer thin, and no longer "ideal." You are not in that idealization of the adolescent. Rather, you are in some sort of wisdom place, or at least the possibility of wisdom, whether that's collective wisdom or one's own wisdom, one's wisdom about oneself. That's what you're entering in the final interlude.

Lee. You hit it! We celebrate adolescence, but we do not celebrate senescence.

Russ. That's correct. In fact, it's not just not celebrated, it's totally devalued.

Lee. You and I are trying to restore the value of senescence.

Russ. Yes. The value of it, the value of aging, what aging makes possible. A focus on all the *new* things possible in one's experience. Obviously, some of the new things have a negative aura, a negative evaluation, like the deterioration of the body. Okay, so that's new, and that's different. It forces one to look at decay directly, to come to realize that the decay we experience in our bodies is part of life. It's not just how decay plays into dying but how we experience decay as a natural part of life's transition to death. I recall seeing some photographs of decayed and dying things of all sorts with the photographs taken at normal range. One could feel the pull to "turn away." But these were then followed by close-up images of the same decay. Stunning! Fascinating! So looking closer, finding a deeper view, even of one's decaying body may yield riches one could not believe would be there.

Lee. Transitions are borderlines.

Russ. They announce a primary task of the final interlude: how to come to terms with all the negatives, the pains, the hurts, the dysfunctions, the losses; how to value this cascade of troubles as a natural part of life. This alone makes it possible to value life even more.

Lee. Precisely. The discovery of epiphanies in the final interlude indicates that the *mind* has not necessarily aged to the same degree as the body. It can be nurtured and cared for and kept vital.

Russ. Yes, for sure. Let's look at some ways in which that can actually happen. Take your dream for example. In the dream, you're introducing to an audience, your "father." In the dream the father is a figure that you don't know and is certainly different than your actual father. As I said earlier, I think it's fair to say this could be your *psychic* father and you're introducing this figure to an audience. Okay now, how would one deal with this dream in terms of all the possibilities inherent in the dream. Not just paying attention to the dream, because the dream's got your attention. To me, the easiest way to get there is to connect with the *story* aspect of the dream.

Lee. Of what it means to be fathered.

Russ. Yes, there's that aspect and what it means to introduce the psychic father to an audience. How do you do that?

Lee. We have had fathers in the journey of life. Some have not been as fortunate. I know from my practice the persistence of looking and seeking after the father. In this there is often loneliness and de-spair. To have a father, to be fathered, is at the heart of mythology

Russ. Yes. And those myths are *stories*. So, if you were to write a story based on the dream you might start with your actual introduction that you were presenting to the audience. And, as you write that, you would start experiencing things that would become the *next* element in the story.

Lee. While you spoke it occurred to me that the person whom I was introducing as my father is clos-er visually to the appearance of my paternal grand-father whom I never met.

Russ. Now that's interesting as it brings in the el-ement of linking the generations, begins to animate issues of lineage. These too are strong story lines. In the dream, do you have a sense of your introducing the father so he's going to say something to the audience?

Lee. I am simply introducing him, that's all I know.

Russ. So, in the dream, we don't know what is *next.* That is the invitational aspect of all dreams.

Lee. What we know as we talk here, is the significance of being fathered.

Russ. Yes, for sure. Currently, we all have our stories of not being fathered. In terms of a person relating to a dream, the dream itself is a source for generating stories we didn't even know were in us. Dream as father, if you will. So the dream becomes an opening for an aging person to not just tell repetitious memories, but to actually tell the story that is being born in the dream, the story that wants to be birthed.

Lee. It has been poignantly brought to my attention how I have fathered various candidates in the academic world. I've been getting letters and acknowledgments from former students thanking me for helping them to make a choice. We father in ways we were not fathered. Is this not true?

Russ. It's true. Another angle on fathering is not just the lineage backwards, but the lineage forward as well. So that the students thanking you now for fathering them are going to be still in the world and making and producing and manifesting and that is part of your lineage. You have a future!

Lee. Well now, if the function of dream in the final interlude is to remind us of the complexity of the lineages that we have established in life that would be very comforting. Wouldn't you agree?

Russ. I think so. If I focus on my ancestry, and really appreciate my ancestry, it has obviously provided me with first of all the reality of being. The fact of my being in the world has come from my ancestry. In relationship to that I think it's very useful for people as they age to know and learn more and more about their ancestors. Because we come out of a long line of ancestors. Knowing what that is, in as much detail as we can, allows us to actually see the gene pool that we came out of, and is responsible for our very being. That's a fundamental fact of some kind, a fundamental reality that is greatly underappreciated. Appreciating this is grist for the final interlude as we grow older. As a kid you are not concerned about this, you couldn't care less. But as you get older, particularly as you get older and older, this stream of history that we come out of becomes more and more meaningful. I find that dreams have a huge part to play in this. My own major experience with this came in a dream. The dream was just an old man telling me that he was my grandfather. Well, I knew my grandfathers, and this figure was not my grandfather. But as I worked with that dream (which I have described elsewhere and has been dramatized in a TV documentary) and followed the "hints" that revealed themselves, what I discovered was that figure in the dream was in fact my grandfather. The person that I had known as my maternal grandfather was not really my grandfather. My mother had not known about this at all. Her mother had told her only as she was dying. She told my mother the truth.[2] My mother's actual father was another man, and that was the man who appeared in my dream. All of this had been kept secret, and my mother kept it secret from my father and from me, my sister and brother. So here's a situation where the dream itself brings about knowledge of one's lineage that one did not consciously know. The dream brings up many issues we can't discuss here. But it clearly highlights the fundamental importance of *actual* lineage. So there is the lineage that one produces into the future of one's family if one has family or produces children even without family (in the case of my true grandfather). There is also the lineage produced in those you have impacted as teacher, all the students and analysands as an ongoing stream into the future of people that you have impacted and because you have impacted them they are going to impact others carrying on something of that psychic genetics into the future. When you say that's comforting I think that is so. One belongs to the world as it goes on even when one is not literally present.

Lee. What comes to mind is the German word for dream, *Traum*. From this we created "trauma." But you were dreaming of a trauma in life that was corrected. No more delusions. You met your grandfather there.

Russ: There' are so many stories that we don't really know that we could find out if we made the effort in terms of people that we are connected to in our lineage. So one task at least I feel is important in my own experience is finding out the stories from people that are in my lineage. To see what kind of stories I came out of. Not just the people I came out of, but the stories, because the stories are as progenitive as the people are. It is vitalizing to get a sense of the stories that what one is *in* as one grew up, the stories that intersected with you in connection with relatives and ancestors. These are powerful things that can be very exciting as one gets older. They are not so much a part of what we do when we are younger, or even in our middle years doing our career and relationships. But as one's ties to those things of the world are loosened, as one enters into the final interlude, the pull of story, at least for me, is becoming very strong. Not just to hear the stories from my lineage, and my own stories from my own past, but also to *tell* stories as they come, and particularly to tell stories that begin in dreams, or in other experiences like synchronicities. As I often say, every synchronicity is a story. If we just stay settled with experiencing a synchronicity and puzzle its meaning, and yes we are impacted and yes it's powerful, but we lose the story quality, the story sense of the synchronicity. It is this enthusiasm for story that I find more and more compelling as I move into the final interlude. We don't follow that through enough. It's so potentially rich.

Lee: Remember that the word *enthusiasm* means "the God within." *Enthusia.* Perhaps in the final interlude, to renew the enthusiasms of life would have a remarkable healing effect. True?

Russ. It can happen, that's for sure. I want to tell you a story that seems to belong here. On one of my trips to Scotland, I wanted to meet with storytellers. Scotland has a history of wandering storytellers such as the tinkers and others and I wanted to meet with some of these people. Why? Because at home nobody tells stories. Where do we really hear or tell stories anymore? We have films and we have books and we can have TV and theater, all these venues. But where you do you really experience person-to-person story telling? It's so rare. One of the reasons why I like working analytically with people is that it is one of the few places where one hears stories now. Moreover, one is prompted to tell stories as well. I'm convinced that this storytelling and story hearing and the *reciprocity* of stories is in itself healing. This can go on in various ways in psychotherapy and is one of the things that creates the healing factor. We don't have many venues in our modern world for actually doing this. Whether the Internet makes it possible, whether the social media and all that is developing at a lightning pace can make genuine story telling "come back" no one knows yet. That story is yet to be told. Part of the reason I wanted to be with storytellers was I wanted to experience that *presence* of someone telling me a story who was a stranger. So, I went to the School of Scottish Studies and I talked to the head man there and he gave me the names of several story-tellers that they had had contact with. Part of their work at the university was to collect stories, make recordings, and publish them in books. It was a monumental academic approach. One of the people he told me about was a guy who was almost 100 years old at that time on the Island of Mull living in a rest home. So I went to the Island of Mull and I found the rest home. I asked to talk to the man I was given the name of. I was led back to his room and we meet and I close the door. He says "it's in the bottom drawer" pointing to the chest next to his bed. So, I open the drawer, and find his bottle. There are a couple of glasses on the chest and in no time at all we were on our way. A highland single malt is a great way to start! So, I ask, "would it be possible for you to tell me some stories?" "Sure," he responds, "I can tell stories." So I set up my tape recorder, turn it on, lean back in my chair next to his bed and I'm full ready to hear and record his stories. But for the longest while he says nothing at all. I say, "Is something wrong?" He beckons me to come closer, I bend down, and he whispers in my ear, "Turn that thing off." As I do this, I see on his bureau a book and I can see that it's the same book that I had been shown at the University—a book of his collected stories. I pick it up, and I say to him, "Ah, I understand. You've already told your stories; they've been published in the book. Yes, I can read them." I start saying thanks for your time and the exquisite dram and he reaches for the book. I give it to him and he gives it a toss so it lands and floor. "Those are not my stories," he says. "My stories are in my ears and in my breath and on my tongue. Those," he said, pointing to the book, "are just words on paper." For the next four hours he told me stories. That experience was one of the high points of my life. Here was a person who was a real storyteller telling the stories in the way that would *matter*. I could read them sure. But without this experience, I could never hear them live in his speaking, his voicing, his telling from what he was hearing, and seeing within his own psyche. Four hours! Finally, he got really tired and fell asleep. It was just remarkable. I was in such an altered state of consciousness myself it took me awhile to realize that *hearing* these things in the way he told them, had a genuinely transformative impact on me. Ever since then, I have known there is a quality of intimacy in the telling of stories and the hearing of stories that creates a field of *otherness* that is incredible, and is in itself very healing—just the *fact* of your participation in it. I went out of that place and I simply walked for a very long time, still in the aura of that experience. It was incredible.

Lee: In the aura of *orality*.

Russ. Indeed. He was almost 100 years old. This was a great gift to me from someone in the final interlude. Part of how I function now is very much due to him. The lineage of his storytelling has impacted me and has worked to transform how I work in my analytic practice, how I am in in my personal life, how I write and create. His lineage lives on into the future, because the people that I impact, whether my family, or in the people I work with, are carrying something of that on into the future. It will be ongoing. And so there's that past lineage and the future lineage. As you get into the depth of the final interlude, both of these lineages are sources of vitality and psychic life that is counterweight to the necessary decay and all the debilitating things that one faces as one gets older.

Lee: Where we might read to be put to sleep, he told stories that allowed him to sleep.

Russ: Imagine sleep after such telling! When in that story mode, he had such vitality. I can only dream that I might know such vitality sometime. I couldn't bear to wake him up and so we never had a proper goodbye. But he knows. He knows what he did for me. So, it's not "good bye." He is surely dead now, but he is still so alive in me. The lineage is alive, like living strands of DNA. I'll never say goodbye to him. The whole experience was instructive to me in a deep way.

Lee: His going to sleep—so powerful a parting. I had a very different experience with someone who became storyteller in Scotland. She eventually married and moved back to the United States and lives now in Colorado. She does a Celtic Festival every year. I went one summer at her invitation to tell fairy tales. Fairytales are not print, but breath. How important this is! And in names too. Your name, Lockhart. What's the story there?

Russ: Well, the *lock* part refers to "lake." The *hart* part refers to the red deer. So, lake of the red deer. Every so often, I'll have a dream picturing some aspect of this "story" of my name. Just recently, not an image of lake, but some cityscape. Into this scene, amidst the usual hubbub of cars and noise, comes this red deer. The Lockhart family motto is *Corda Serrata Pando:* "I open locked hearts."

Lee: The spirit of your lineage!

Russ. Yes, alive. Something about the animal spirit of Lockhart came into this dream. I am trying to park on the street to go into my house and I can see my dream house which is not my house. But it is my house in the dream, set in a wooded area. The house is covered with red ceramic tiles. I'm looking at these tiles which are very striking to me, while trying to find a suitable place to park. There is no place to park, so I move on up to the intersection. I'm looking in my rearview mirror and I see someone pull out, so I start backing up in order to get this parking space. For some reason, I stop the car and I look over to my left and there's a deer, a red deer standing there a few yards away. I get out of the car and I am drawn to be with the deer. I walk up to the deer and I stroke the deer's neck. He does not run away. He responds to my petting like a horse does. I turn and look back at my car and I see it is being towed away. I shout out, "No, no! I live here." And I point to my house, and once again the red tiles catch my attention. Every so often I have a dream like this where the red deer appears. When this deer appears I know something about the Lockhart clan, the Lockhart lineage, the Lockhart whatever it is, is "up." As I get older now, a dream like this is very exciting. And very enlivening. I find myself all stirred up by the presence of this deer. This kind of experience convinces me that as people get older if they would pay attention to their dreams this would naturally lead to paying attention to *why* it's older memories that are so strongly a part of the aging experience. These older memories want to be *storied*. This is not just idle memory, it's not just a sign of advancing dementia. It's a call to story your life before it ends. Paying attention to dreams is going to encourage better remembering. Even in fairly advanced states of dementia people will still have dreams. They can still attend, they can still be with the dreams, participate with the dream. To me, the dream is always good medicine. Even if it's a night-mare it is still good medicine because the dream is connecting you with something you can't get connected to otherwise.

Lee: There is a double pun in that dream. I ask my analysands not to refer to cars as cars, but to use the term "auto mobile," that which gives you self-mobility. The self-mobility is not what you're driving, but the life that is standing there to greet you. You stroke it. That is your lineage. It's gorgeous. I've noted particularly since my accident, something disconcerting at first. Right up to today, I'm referring to dreams that are *hallucinatory*, that is, I'm awake, but there are individuals present in the room. I'm wondering what they are doing here in the room. A moment passes and then I'm in the reality of the morning. Have you had such hallucinatory dreams?

Russ. Oh, yes. Fairly often actually and more so as I get older.

Lee: Thank you. Now here is a thing we need to discuss: the power of the hallucinatory dream. As you and I have gotten older this has been an experience for us and it's very compelling!

Russ Yes, I have to agree, they are very compelling. Again, it seems to me this is more common in people who pay attention to their dreams, deeply engaged with their dreams. It is as if being engaged with dreams opens more dimensions of experience.

Lee: Dream life and regular life come together.

Russ Yes. To my mind this is another benefit of what can happen when you pay attention to your dreams and even more so as you get older, this inter-penetration.

Lee: I think writing on the hallucinatory dream is critically important.

Russ: Okay, I can agree with that. What's an example?

Lee: Individuals who are in the house tend to greet me in one way or another. This is the first time I have told or spoken to anyone about that power of the hallucinatory dream. I'm not certain I can explain it other than what I have said to you.

Russ: The way I experience it in most instances that I would relate to this idea of the hallucinatory dream, is the persistence of the dream state into waking in such a way that when I'm awake just on the other side of the transition from sleeping to waking the figures are still there. I'm fully awake and yet I'm seeing this figure over there in the corner. It's not a lucid dream because I am awake not asleep. It is as if the dream is awake in me as well. Then over a period of moments or sometimes longer, it fades. But it's there! I'm uncomfortable calling it a hallucination, partly because we tend to think of hallucinations as *unreal*, while my sense of these experiences is that they are very real, extraordinarily real. Whatever that figure is, it is there.

Lee: The dream *in* life.

Russ: For the moment, the veil between dreaming and waking is porous, it is not a disjunctive state. It is continuous. That figure has come into my conscious experience. It has persisted through the dream state and on into my waking experience. It is a very powerful experience. It can make your hair on the back of your neck stand up, it can send shivers through your body. But I have never encountered a figure yet in these experiences that I want to go away or to avoid. Indeed, I want to connect. I have a desire to connect.

Lee: I have had the feeling they want to connect to me.

Russ: Yes, and it is reciprocal. I haven't had an experience where it's a horrific presence or something that scares me. It's more a sense of *camaraderie*. It's always a very unusual experience. This is not something one talks about too openly. On the other hand, why not? We are old enough now.

Lee: At 88, here in the period of the final interlude, the dream world and my inner world meet in my outer world.

Russ: It's an unusual topic. It is not talked about. I'm convinced because of my experience and others' experience that this is a very intriguing kind of reality. I've only experienced it as I've gotten older, not something I experienced when I was younger. It may have something to do with a capacity that *requires* aging. People are more likely to think of it as a brain malfunction, but I think not.

Lee: I feel gratefully empowered by sharing this with you. And you have had them too! It will be interesting to hear from others about their experience of "others." The final interlude can be characterized by a tension between deterioration of body and mind and the re-creation of mental energies that sustain and frame daily life.

Russ: I like your use of the word re-creation there because the other sense of that is recreation which implies play. I think one of the most seriously underrated aspects of aging is the necessity to develop or re-develop a sense of play as one gets older. When we are kids, nobody teaches us how to play. We know how to play from the beginning. We just play. It comes naturally and it's part of our being human—may even have had a role to play in our *becoming* human. *Homo ludens.* We come into the world that way and until school beats it out of us, we know how to play. Once school gets hold of us, then play becomes problematical. "Older age" is often called a second childhood. Would that it were so!

Lee: It's a time of re-discovery of one's child-like spontaneities.

Russ: To recapture the sense of play is one of the ways of re-creating and recreating the mind and the psyche while undergoing these tensions of aging.

Lee: And that must be why psyche creates these

in-life dreams. I don't know what else to call them. Because they demand play, a *ludic* approach.

Russ: I couldn't agree more. To play with these experiences rather than think one has a diseased mind. And look at the double aspect of play. We use the word play for playing like children do. And then we use play for drama, whether tragedy or comedy. This tragedy/comedy aspect of aging is, paradoxically, one way of playing. Quite literally, being able to articulate the sense of tragedy, being able to articulate the sense of comedy, and the interaction between them. This is priceless. Think of George Burns and how he used comedy in relationship to aging. It kept him going. Norman Cousins, when he had cancer and was in the hospital, he discovered that if he watched comedians, and played these comic programs over and over, that his healing was speeded up. He felt so much better. The psychic response became enlivened. Research shows that as you develop these kinds of problems, the plethora of body problems as you get older, the quality of your state of mind, the quality of your current psychic presence in relationship to your body, becomes part of the healing process. If you're full of bitterness and loss you are actually undermining your own healing process. But if you fill yourself up with some sense of play, some sense of the tragic-comic dimension of your experience, and build play into your daily life, to put your psyche into that place of play, it will impact not only your resilience in the face of decline, but will enhance the body's healing potential. This sense of play can not only produce its own healing power, but it can recruit the natural healing mechanisms of the body, even when the body is in decline. Play, in all senses, will not keep you from dying, will not keep your body from falling apart, but it will certainly keep your psychic mind alive and you will be able to deal with the vicissitudes of aging in more productive ways. Play is crucial!

Lee. Related to this is the capacity to celebrate—*homo festivus*—ever so quietly, or anticipatorily. Homo sapiens, homo faber, homo ludens, homo festivus. The quaternity of our being human. Thinking, working, playing, and celebrating. They work best when they work together and not as separates, as things apart. It is crucial to carry this on to whatever degree one can as one ages.

Russ. Recent brain research is very exciting in relation to aging. It had been thought that neurogenesis (the generation of new brain cells) came to an end and then deteriorated from then on. It has now been discovered that this is not so, that neurogenesis occurs right up to the moment of death.

Lee. And let's remember, that death can be a revelatory experience!

Russ. Yes. So one of the things that greatly impacts the eroding effects of dementias, is the increase in neurogenesis. Part of growing old means that one needs to undertake activities and ways of being and doing that further and enhance neurogenesis. There are several things under one's control to achieve this as one ages. A foundational one, is sleeping well. I would broaden this and say sleeping *and* dreaming well is going to produce new brain cells—even in the aging brain.

Lee. In consciousness, we call "dreaming" imagination. In sleep, we call it dreaming.

Russ. The importance of what you've just noted is that the waking imagination, the waking dream, also enhances neurogenesis. One recent study took a group of concert level pianists divided into two groups. As you know, anyone who's at the concert level practices a great deal, spends many hours a day practicing in order to stay at that level. As aging sets in, they start losing some of that capacity. But in the study what happened was this. One group continued to practice in the way they ordinarily practiced every day, several hours a day, doing all the things concert level pianists do in their practicing. The other group stopped physical practice and simply spent the same amount of time *imagining* that they were practicing. They would visualize and imagine the feel of their fingers playing. They would get into a deeply imaginal meditative state, and they would be practicing "in their mind." The researchers then measured the brain activity of these two groups. They found that the people who had been imagining actually had more neurogenesis than the people who had been practicing physically. What this points to, and what is so critical for our finding ways of "aging well," is this. Habits, those repeated patterns of behavior we give no thought to but just do, do not generate neurogenesis. Habits are essential in terms of being efficient and spending the least amount of energy doing things that need to be repeated. The problem is, that as one gets older the habit patterns take over one's life. One spends all of one's time in habits. But habits don't generate neurogenesis; but imagination does. So you've got to spend more time imagining. Our brain is actively "imagining" during dreaming sleep and when we wake up, we need to engage actively in imagination as well. Imagining, then, becomes a necessary skill for aging well. The things that stimulate the imagination are stories, the potential for dreams to generate stories, the potential for becoming aware of one's lineage, going backwards and going forwards. One can imagine how all these people that you affected as teacher, as fathering them in that way, you can imagine how they are going to contribute to things in the future. You can imagine all these ways and more. And as you are imagining, your brain is developing more brain cells and this is one of the natural mechanisms of inhibiting dementia. So one serves oneself a great function by engaging the imagination. Very powerful!

Lee. I had a telephone conversation with my former wife, whose current husband had been a writer for the *Los Angeles Times*. He's now in his 90s, and is slowly ebbing away with a chronic disease. I asked about him and she replied that it was only a matter of time before he passed, but she added, at the moment he's playing the piano. I exclaim, "Wonderful! It is the most psychologically healing thing he could do at the moment." This is a brilliant example of how an individual can seek the syntonic and overcome, however chronic, the dystonic.

Ral. Great example! In my experience, when I was a teenager, I got pretty good at playing the piano, up to the recital level. Then I decided to stop, partly because I discovered girls, and they got my attention. My mother warned me that I would regret this. At the time, I didn't regret it at all. I had fun playing the piano, but it was also filled with those hours practicing, and anxiety about performance. So I willingly gave it up. Now, nearing 80, I have the piano that I had as a child. I used to be able to play Chopin pretty well. Now, when I try to play Chopin, my fingers remember Chopin. They remember. I can feel it in my fingers. They remember what to do and I have a kind of ghost sensation of playing as I used to do. But, of course, I can't make my fingers do that ghost performance. My fingers literally won't do what they remember. Now I can use that experience as a way of stopping and walking away from the piano forever. But how can I *play* with this frustration? I can't play what I did before. But I can play simpler things. One composer I like a great deal is Eric Satie. His piano compositions are simple enough for me to play and start having fun again. I can make my fingers do it. When I discovered this, there was such joy! I was so pleased! Then I thought of my mom's warning. Yes, mom, you were absolutely right, as you were in so many things I disregarded. But I'm back, regret tempered with joy.

Lee. My story is a little different. I too got to the recital stage and was heading on to the concert level. I wanted more than anything to learn to play the organ, so I took organ lessons in San Diego and practiced at my mother's church. I loved the sound of the organ. I went to Radio Shack and bought a keyboard that had organ sounds. I played mostly church organ in electronic form. I find playing Bach interludes, organ interludes, profoundly healing. While the fingers may not be as supple as they were, they create incredible music all the same. For you, Eric Satie; for me, the organ. I have a collection of keyboard music by Alexander Schreiner, the organist for the Mormon Church. I can set the keyboard for organ to play his incredible music. The upshot is, "Do not be hampered by limitation, live with the limitations and do what calls to you." You found Eric Satie; I found the healing power of organ music with an organ keyboard set up in my home. I love it. In a sense, you and I are playing theme and variations.

Russ. Your mentioning not being stopped by limits is an incredible piece of advice to people who are getting older and starting to experience limits. Sometimes we don't experience limits until we get older, but sooner or later everyone starts bumping into limits. The most common response to limits is to get stopped, which goes into the feeling of loss, and this creates a downward spiral into depression and that becomes bitterness. There's nothing that's harder on the psyche than bitterness. It's very destructive. It's pure poison. But just as you can improvise your music, so too you can you improvise with bitterness. Playing bitter music. Writing out the bitterness as a song, a poem, a story. Speaking the bitterness out loud. In other words, *any* form of expression becomes the possibility of imagination and play—even bitterness. Research is finding that it is *expression*—the actual *doing* of something from inner to outer— that is one of the strongest factors exciting neurogenesis. We know that habit diminishes neurogenesis. Think about school. When they start cutting the budget, what gets cut first is all forms of expression, while all forms of habit, such as rote learning, rote memorization, all that stuff is what remains. We are literally killing children's brains by taking away expression. When you're expressing, whether it's singing, dancing, writing, acting, playing a musical instrument, beating on drums—you are increasing neurogenesis, re-creating and recreating and vitalizing your brain. As we get old it becomes a challenge to express ourselves. If you sit there in an envelope of bitterness you are dying more rapidly. Instead, you can use the bitterness to express, you can turn your bitterness into a soliloquy and express it forcefully. Read it out loud, act it out, portray different characters obsessed with bitterness. The ways of expression are endless. If older people and their caregivers would focus on expression, it would revolutionize how people grow old. To develop faith in the value of expression of our inner world as we age, is powerful medicine, an *elixir*!

Lee. Expressing can be found in singing, uttering, playing the keyboard—so many ways. I can sit at the organ keyboard and play the music of Alexander Schreiner and have an overwhelming sense of well-being. Music expresses the ineffable in psyche. You can't describe what is being expressed, but you can feel the power of it.

Russ. Indeed. In fact, when you are expressing, one of the reasons why it's so beneficial for neurogenesis, is that it is impacting you on many different levels: thought, feeling, emotion, sensation. It's *not* abstracting yourself from experience, not just the thinking about doing, but the doing. Descartes had it wrong. It's not "I think, therefore I am." It's, "I do, therefore I am." When we just go mental, just asking what something means, or to interpret it, or only to understand it, we are "in our heads" as the expression goes. No wonder dementias are so feared, because most of what we do as we grow older is fall into whirlpools of fearful thought. Dementia will begin to destroy thought. But expression, as a basis for increasing neurogenesis, can keep dementia at bay.

Lee. Even thinking, as defines our character as Homo sapiens, becomes an "antidote" if it goes into an outer expression. We must create and express, as we can, meaning as we are able to do.

Russ. And everyone can do something. You may not be able, because of physical limitations, to get up and do a jig. But you can sit in your wheelchair and jiggle your arms. It's just too bad that there seems to be so little awareness of these necessities of expression. One can always reconnect with childhood by remembering experiences as a kid, as well as dreams as a kid. Listen to my childhood repeating dream. I was walking home from school and all the houses on the block looked exactly like my home. I would go in one and it turned out not to be my home. I had that dream from the time I started school until just before my teens. I never found my home. We know that repeating dreams from childhood create a leitmotif for one's life. I can describe my life through the lens of this dream. At the beginning, everything I try feels like home. But sooner or later I discover it is not home—just like my childhood dream. I'm nearing 80 now, and I start thinking about dying. Where would my "dying at home" occur in the deepest sense? Everyone I've talked to about this wants to "die at home." Of course, dying "at home" makes death itself a certain kind of home. This creates a question of what has been, what have I experienced as the deepest sense of home—given my childhood dream of never finding home? This is a multifaceted idea because one can feel at home in one's literal house. One can feel quite at home in one's literal body. I know what that feels like and I know the painful thing aging is that one starts to feel the body is no longer "home." Still, at homeness is important. What I came to realize is that I never have found some outer thing that really functioned in the deepest sense as "home." Where do I feel at home now? What I have discovered is this: where I feel truly and deeply at home is in the dream. I can't describe this in any other way. So that's the answer to my childhood dream. I have stopped looking outside for home. I have found it inside. And the most inside is the dream. When I wake up from a dream I have this feeling of having stepped out of my home. It is a very peculiar feeling but so very strong.

Lee. In sharing your dream, you invite others into your home.

Russ. To be sure. My interview published in Rob

Henderson's book on "enterviews" with Jungian analysts is titled, "Listen to the Dreams."[21] Now you know why. Before that book was published, I had a dream in which a voice told me simply: "Not interviews, but enterviews." When I told Rob this dream, he decided to subtitle the volume, "'Enterviews' with Jungian Analysts." I'm glad you brought that up. I think this is the first time I've said this out loud. I tell people all the time to say or read things that are important out loud so that it goes in one's ears as well as in one's eyes. What happens in your brain is different than what happens when things come only through the eyes. Imagine the difference between reading a musical score through your eyes, and listening to that score through your ears. I like to tell my dream to myself *out loud*, because of this same principle. So in hearing a dream or a poem, speaking it out loud, particularly if you've got the dream or poem "in your bones" to use Kim Rosen's[22] wonderful image, is to experience that extraordinary resonant quality that ripples through your whole body. The bodyness produced by out loudness is itself a kind of medicine—and for us oldsters, it can be a genuine tonic!

Lee. When I was in graduate school and doing my Master's degree at Northwestern, Robert Frost was one of our major poets for study and *Birches* was a major poem in my textbook.

When I see birches bend to left and right
Across the lines of straighter darker trees,
I like to think some boy's been swinging them.
But swinging doesn't bend them down to stay
As ice-storms do.

This was all in the body. Between my Masters and
my doctorate, I taught at the University of Vermont.
There I had two experiences that changed my life.
One was meeting Dylan Thomas and the other was
listening to Robert Frost's reading his own poetry.
I had never heard the New England accent in the
poem. Of course, I had "translated" the poem into
my own voice. But I heard the poem through his
own voice, it was a different language. You cannot
"see" that experience on a page. It's a different experience altogether—a crucial and valuable difference.

Russ. Let's talk about our current experience in
relationship to death and dying and then turn to
the question of particular things we want to do,
to accomplish, finish or begin in the time we have
left. What is animating us in our immediate future
before the final interlude reaches its final point?

Lee. I follow the obituaries in the *New York Times*.
I experience very powerfully the presence of the
70s, 80s, 90s, and 100s. What fascinates me and is
most moving in these obituaries is that so many of
them have been entertainers, singers, dramatists, and
actors. I am acutely aware of time being *marked* by

their passing, the passing of those whom we do not know personally, but nonetheless have impacted our lives. The deaths of others are time markers in our own lives. This feels critically important to me as I age on.

Russ. I don't read the obituary column of the *New York Times*, but I do read the obituaries in our local newspaper, *The Everett Herald*. One will not find the famous in these page as one does on the larger stage in New York. I find myself without intention looking at the local obituaries, looking at the pictures, reading the stories. I imagine myself knowing this person. Sometimes I have the impulse to contact somebody in the family to find out more about the person because the obituary sparks something particular or peculiar in my mind. If I were to name it, it would have something to do with "story," perhaps unfinished stories. Death always leaves unfinished stories. Every morning, I find myself spontaneously doing this. To me this is very interesting. I am aware from news on the Internet or TV, that there is a focus on celebrity. It is a marking of time—a kind of clock. The deaths of celebrities become markers not just in a collective sense, but in a more personal sense as well. Part of our collective consciousness is the way celebrities have become woven into the fabric of our life. So when someone dies who is well known and has been part of one's growing up, part of one's consciousness, these passings become *mark-*

ers and harbingers of finality. I know when I hear
the news of someone dying that I have had some
relationship with over the years in terms of their
music or writing or whatever, I experience a "charge"
that shoots through me. They were a part of me. I
am aware of certain parts of me dying through the
vehicle of that figure. I think the story impulse is to
keep something going.

Lee. It is a dying of the "stars" of the heavens, one
by one going out. I've brought the *New York Times*
for June 7 (2015), to show you an article that impressed me. Their stories are about love late in life,
desire and faith, abrupt transitions, and creating.
This is a group of New Yorkers 85 and above, growing ever more numerous in our culture. I have almost finished the autobiography of Oliver Sachs as
well as his article, "The Joy of Turning 80." Imagine:
the *joy* of turning eighty, not the remorse of turning
eighty, but to be in that final interlude with joy!

Russ. This is particularly poignant because in our
culture there is such a heavy emphasis on *youth.*
Trying to stay youthful, trying to look youthful, as
if aging were not natural. Part of what's happening
through the efforts of people like Oliver Sachs, is
a speaking out in ways that are shocking. To talk
about the joy of 80, is shocking to the youth culture,
because the youth culture sees oldsters as done, finished. Get out of view, go away, and die already! To
be present in a very strong way with a sense of joy of

turning 80, that is extraordinary.

Lee. What I have experienced in lecturing on the final interlude to both lay and professional groups, is an energy I didn't realize I was bringing forth, welcoming this stage of our lives, and celebrating it! "Celebrating" is rooted in celebrity. Not living through, but living from. This is a major difference. Youth lives through celebrity.

Russ. When I was an analyst in Los Angeles, I worked with quite a few people who were in the realm of celebrity and without exception I can say that one of the strongest characteristics of their personal experience was fearing the death of their celebrity—even more than their own personal death. Maintaining their celebrity, maintaining that collective energy and visibility that is generated from the collective, became more important than life itself. There was a desperation to hang on to that because that's what they experienced as being alive, as life. As celebrity started to fray in one form or another, a horrible depression would seep into their experience and they had to work strongly against that. The pull of drugs, alcohol, and all sorts of addictions was almost impossible to resist.

Lee. That seems to be the significance of the literature of the final interlude. It's not about depression, it's about expression.

Russ. Exactly. There must be something about getting over a "hump," getting over that dependency on the collective or dependency on the narcissistic aspect of all the input from the collective. This is required to get to that point where you can freely express yourself *as* yourself.

Lee. I am finding that to be true.

Russ. I am too, and I'm still a young chicken!

Lee. No, I think you are an aging rooster!

Russ. OK. I'll accept that.

Lee. In all the books that I have read on aging and helping the aging to remain creative, it is that unfolding of *expression* that is everything. How little this is made part of the care and treatment of the aging!

Russ. There have been three times in my life when I was very close to death. The first time was when I was eight years old. I was a Cub Scout out on a weekend adventure with my cub-pack, taking a hike on a mountain. We were horsing around and I got knocked off the path and I started tumbling down off the path and I was getting pretty banged up from bumping into rocks and bushes but I kept rolling down. At a certain point I experienced the presence of a very large owl in the sky and the owl told me to hang on to the tree. Just at that point I crashed into this smallish tree and I just grabbed onto it and held tight. This tree was at the edge of a cliff and if I'd gone any further I would have fallen over the cliff and died. No question. That was my first experience coming close to dying. I was saved by the vision.

Lee. The message of the owl for you at 77, is to hang on!

Russ. Yes, when I start tumbling down the hill now…

Lee. Hang on! That is the language of our authors as well. That certainly is the language of those couples at 85. My near experience with death came in 2013, when I collapsed walking back from the gas station where I had left the car to be serviced. It was a very hot day and I got to the top of the hill near my home and just collapsed. My next-door neighbor is a doctor who just happened to be there. He staunched my wounds. I also knocked out my front teeth by falling. But it was being in the intensive care ward of the University of Washington hospital where I was taken that struck me to the core. I was put in one of those metal cribs in which you cannot move. One afternoon the head of internal medicine came with a flock of students to each crib and finally turned to me and asked if I had anything to say. I said yes. "Give hope. Give hope, when you come. It is not helpful to be surrounded by a group of students who are viewing an end and not a transformation." He came over and said, "Thank you. Thank you." This was a great day. I don't know what prompted me to be so articulate, but I began to recover from that moment and was soon taken home.

Russ. It sounds like it was very good that you spoke up. This is a key idea too, to speak up. To speak out. Expression!

Lee. Or, to put it another way, once you hear the owl, you must *do* something about it. This is at the center—the *doing*. That is the aging issue of creativity and transformation. I think that is the significance of this work that we are doing. That we are giving hope.

Russ. One of the things I gleaned from the owl vision is the absolute presence of something *other* than my normal consciousness. I was only 8 at that time. Even so, the experience made such an impression on me that from that day on I have had this strong sense of the value of something *other* that's available in one's experience. I know that nearly 70 years later this is going to be a powerful factor in how I go through the final interlude.

Lee. Precisely, because you want to go through it with a syntonic fullness and the presence of "something other" is going to be a crucial part of that.

Russ. The second near-death experience I had was when I was 17. A friend of mine and I were at the Grand Canyon and we decided to hike down to the river on the canyon floor. We thought nothing of doing this, what's a few miles hike to 17-year-olds. We were dressed in Bermuda shorts, tennis shoes, and no shirts. It was early summer just after school. So we go loping down the trail, on down to the Colorado River. It didn't take us all that long to get down there and we played and splashed around in the river for some hours. Then it got to be time to come up. Well, coming up the Grand Canyon is a whole lot different than going down—even for teens. We made it up to the first mile outpost area and we were really exhausted. If I remember right, it was at this point where the park ranger had his cabin. We asked if there was a way we could get some mules or horses to take us the rest of the way up. We were pretty tired. He said no that it was against the rules. We spent the next many hours getting to the next outpost. When we got there we were totally fried. We could go no further. We had no choice but to simply lay down on the path. I was fully aware that laying down on this path was very dangerous because one could roll off and there were snakes. I remember at some point in the night hearing snakes—or was it a dream? In any event, I couldn't move. So I spent the time in a strange state of consciousness thinking that my life was over. But what did that mean? What is a 17-year old's reflections on dying? At the time it was scary, but in retrospect superficial. I was so out of it that I couldn't even think straight.

Lee. Gives you compassion. I think what you're elaborating here is something your daughter also experienced in a very different rhythm and had no vision. Your remarkable experience in the Grand

Canyon presaged another event which would happen many years later in the life of your family. So you can have compassion, profound compassion.

RL. Yes, I think so. I think so because when we woke up in the morning we were 17-year-olds who recovered quickly. We woke up and we felt refreshed. We lurched up the last leg of the trail laughing all the way. At the restaurant we gorged ourselves on breakfast and immediately got sick. But what I remember reflecting on after waking up, before actually getting up on my feet, was *I'm alive!* And then, the question followed: Why? Why am I alive? That question settled so sharply into my mind and body, even now, it's always in the background not far away from my consciousness. Why am I alive?

Lee. Well the key in your observation is: Wake up!

Russ. Yes. Wake up! No matter how bad things are, wake up!

Lee. That was my experience in the hospital: wake up! That admonition is central to living fully in the final interlude.

Russ. I agree. So the presence of "something other" and the question of "why am I alive?" has shadowed everything since. Is this the answer? Getting married, having kids, one accomplishment after another…are these *answers*? Partially, yes. All those things are part of the answer, but never fully the answer.

Lee. That is why our work on the final interlude can be summarized as *waking up*. Waking up to *new* possibilities. There was an article in the *New York Times*, an obituary of a woman 115 years old who died. She had money problems in her last years. All she could eat were the yolks of eggs. But those eggs were transitional objects that kept her going through her 115th year. Imagine that! Our work in the final interlude is answering all those moments in our past that went unarticulated, but are now waking up.

Russ. The third time that I came close to dying followed going to my doctor for my annual check-up. Everything seemed to be fine. I spontaneously raised the question of whether I should have a treadmill test as sort of a baseline because of the heart history of my family and because I never had a treadmill test. My doctor said it was up to me. He didn't seem to be pushing the idea. It was up to me. In that moment I was in a struggle trying to de-cide. I had an intuitive experience, a voice that said, "Do it!" So, I said yes. It was arranged. After the test, I got a call from the cardiologist saying that he wanted to do another test because there were some abnormalities in my results. A nuclear stress test was arranged where radioactive dye is injected and you have some imaging of your heart done before and after a treadmill test. The results showed that some-thing was seriously wrong. The doctor arranged an immediate angiogram which showed that all of my heart arteries were dangerously blocked. I was put into the first available operating room and underwent a quintuple bypass. Later, in talking with the surgeon, he told me that without the operation, I would have had no more than a month to live. The whole experience was a total shock because I had no symptoms. It's called "silent heart disease." If I had not listened to the intuitive voice that said "Do it," I would have died. It was not my consciousness that saved me, but my listening to what "the other" had said. This voice is another example of "wake up." Because I listened, I'm still here after 15 years of having that experience. So, when I think of entering the final interlude, all the things that I've learned from these prior near-death experiences become very prominent. These are my particular ways of entering into the final interlude in the deepest possible way. Thus, paying attention to visions, paying attention to what happens when you really give up, and what comes afterwards, when you let go of everything ego and see what happens. That's the message of the Grand Canyon. The importance of *listening* to that little soft voice in the background saying something—that saved my life. These things are to be big factors in my final interlude.

Lee. You're ready.

Russ. When you're in the final interlude, one becomes more aware of the value of *time*; every moment of time seems to weigh more than it did in earlier experience. It starts having a density, a palpability of some kind that was totally absent when one was younger. Time takes on these qualities that are present in one's consciousness now and literally cannot be ignored. It is impossible to get back into that younger and earlier frame of mind. I'm aware of this when I wake up in the morning—acutely aware. If I wake up with a dream, do I spend time with the dream, or something else? Because of *time*, it becomes a weighty decision. I'm thinking of *Zorba the Greek*, when Zorba talked about grocers having to weigh everything. As I approach the final interlude, this weighing becomes a constant activity.

Lee. Consider that the final interlude is the 80s, 90s and 100s. That's possibly 25 more years for you. You've described what happened at 17, and here you are approaching 77, entering the final interlude.

Russ. I feel pretty strongly that the near-death experiences I've had and the weight that I have given them, has been a preparation for whatever is coming. I don't think I would have gotten this in any other way. Like it or not, one is going to be entering the final interlude. One can have all kinds of hopes about how that's going to be and to work out. But the day to day hints about what's *important* stand out to me.

Lee. For you, entering the final interlude is standing at the edge of a Grand Canyon.

Russ. I can buy that metaphor.

Lee. It's very personal to you. I cannot say that.

Russ. What I'm starting to experience on the edges of my experience are what I will call "hints" and "intimations" about things to *do* or reflect on or to be aware of. These things are like sparks from a fire: they are there but when you really look at them you can't find them. They disappear quickly, these sparks, but I believe they are important. They are the presence of something that's on the edge of experience. To me, these are important *potentials*, something that can crystalize in the final interlude if one can catch hold of them and bring them into manifestation. It feels like it has everything to do with what is going to be crucial in my experience of the final interlude. Of course, I would put dreams, and intuitions, and the presence of "otherness" in this category. So I'm feeling an optimism, if that's the right word. Most definitely an *enthusiasm*. To some it may seem weird to be talking about being enthusiastic when entering the final interlude.

Lee. To be responsive to the god within!

Russ. These sparks come up in all manner of different ways; they can strike at any time. They can strike when I wake up; they strike when I'm trying to do something else or focused on something else; strike me when I'm working on taxes, paying bills, or whatever. *Something* is calling me, calling my attention to something else than what I'm immediately focused on. *If* I can pay attention—which is what my earlier experiences all seem to have in common. This paying attention to the *presence* of otherness requires letting go of ego. If I can do that, then it feels like what I want to experience and to do before I die, will be possible.

Lee. May I point out it is happening. You are in it. You are doing it.

Russ. Thank you Lee. Just sitting here with you sparks so much. It is such a joy.

EPILOGUE
Lee Roloff

The primary tasks of living in the final interlude are to attend to the complexities of inner mental challenges, to the physical demands, and to fulfilling as much creativity in word and deed as dictated by circumstances.

Of paramount concern in this work has been a sensitivity to its potentially divergent readers: those living in the final interlude; those family and friends who care for those in the final interlude; and, of course, the psychological and other professionals serving those living in their eighties and beyond.

All readers should recognize the importance of Oliver Sacks and his emphasis on the mental life of the aging, and his call to vitalize the *connection* to both the outer *and* the inner world.

Every individual faces the unexpected, the accidental, the changes in cultural life, and the myriad yet unknown matters that will challenge the very essence, quality, and demands with which we all must contend. We hope that *The Final Interlude* will provide techniques and approaches that encourage individuals to live on. Alternatives are many; stubbornness to change is a most unfortunate condition. Live well. Die well.

EPILOGUE

Russ Lockhart

The great communion to which we all belong is the communion of dying and death. No matter what our lot in life has been, we all share this common fate.

The deepest and oldest meaning of the root from which communion grows (*mei-*[1]) is "to change," and "to go." Death is the profoundest change of all. And since humans were humans and perhaps before, the end brings the question: "where do we *go* from here when we die"?

No matter what our belief or its absence, this question insists on itself, not as an ego question, but one that rises from the depths. This question cannot be answered and so it becomes the great unanswerable. It is this not being able to *know* that makes this question such a mystery. But not knowing creates uncertainty and uncertainty is generally noxious to us humans. Religions have been mankind's major ways of reducing this uncertainty. People find great comfort in "knowing" that they will go to heaven, or whatever form of "after life" one adheres to, or, strangely, a kind of comfort in "knowing" there is no going anywhere at all. All this "answers" uncertainty, but we each know in our own way, there is no answer at all.

Psychotherapy and analysis is like the confessional; you hear the most intimate things and there is nothing more intimate than one's death. Lee and I have been privy to these intimacies, both of us overawed by these confrontations with the death and dying of others, as we edge ever closer to our own. The final interlude in the last analysis is a time of preparation for our leaving our life, our leaving this world. Lee and I have presented at least a taste of what we consider to be the deepest way into such preparation. We trust that the hints we have articulated will encourage the reader to approach the final interlude as a journey, a journey with an unknown destination, an unknown time of arrival, an unknown unlike any other. *Bon voyage!*

END NOTES

1. C. G. Jung. *Memories, Dreams, Reflections.* New York: Vintage Books, 1989.

2. David Lehman (Ed.) *Oxford Book of American Poetry.* Oxford: Oxford University Press, 2006.

3. The terms "syntonic" and "dystonic" were developed by Eric Erikson and Joan Erikson in their book, *The Life Cycle Completed.* New York: W.W. Norton and Company, 1997.

4. Douglas Thomas & John Seely Brown. "Learning for a World of Constant Change." Presented at the 7th Glion Colloquium, University of Southern-California, June 2009.

5. Johan Huizinga. *Homo Ludens.* Boston: Beacon Press, 1955.

6. The writer is indebted to a special section on "Retirement," published in *The New York Times,* March 15, 2014. A notable piece by Phyllis Korkki, "The Science of Older and Wiser," explores the possibilities of personal wisdom by reference to the work of Erik Erikson and his wife Joan Erikson.

7. Ibid., 7.

8. Ibid., 8.

9. Benedict Carey. "Older Mind May Just Be a Fuller Mind," Science Section, *The New York Times*, January 28, 2014, p.3.

10. C.G. Jung. *Memories, Dreams, Reflections.* New York: Vintage Books, 1989.

11. Marc C. Agronin. *How We Age: A Doctors Journey into the Heart of Growing Old.* Philadelphia: Da Capo Press, 2011.

12. _____ . *Therapy with Older Clients: Key Strategies for Success.* New York: W. W. Norton and Company, 2010.

13. Ibid., 44-57.

14. Ibid., 266.

15. Ibid., 259, in which the neologism "gerotranscendence" is cited, 61.

16. John Hill. *At Home in the World: Sounds and Symmetries of Belonging.* New Orleans: Spring Journal Books, 2010.

17. Ibid., 13.

18. Russell A. Lockhart. *Words as Eggs: Psyche in Language and Clinic.* Everett: The Lockhart Press, 2012.

19. Emily Dickinson. "Astra Castra." In Richard B. Sewall, *The Life of Emily Dickinson*. Cambridge: Harvard University Press, 1974, 576 (second stanza). I quote her original versing and punctuation in favor of the modern reconstruction.

20. C. G. Jung. *Modern Man in Search of a Soul.* New York: Harcourt, Brace & World, Inc. , 1965.

21. Russell Arthur Lockhart. "Listen to the Dreams." Robert and Janice Henderson (Eds.). *Living with Jung: 'Enterviews' with Jungian Analysts.* New Orleans: Spring Journal Books, 2006.

22. Kim Rosen. *Saved by a Poem: The Transformative Power of Words*. Carlsbad: Hay House, Inc., 2009.

ABOUT THE AUTHORS

Lee Roloff was born in San Diego, California, in 1927, and died in Seattle, Washington, in 2015. He received his B.A. from San Diego State University (Speech), his M.A. from Northwestern (Literature), and his Ph.D. from the University of Southern California (Communication). He began his illustrious teaching career at Occidental College, followed by Southern Methodist University and fully flowering in many directions, becoming full professor of Interpretation at Northwestern University. He was distinguished for his work in performance and for his ability to inspire students to bring imagination and depth of feeling to poetry, drama, and theater. These talents were to find further elaboration and depth in his later career as a Jungian analyst. He was known for his care and concern and depth of feeling for those who sought his guidance. His book, *The Perception and Evocation of Literature* (1973), is a classic in the arts of criticism. He was a poet of rare sensibilities, a lecturer who inspired and animated audiences, and a man who was always present with the warmth of his attention, the acuity of his insights, and compassion for differences of all kinds. Summing up his life is difficult, but I think my dream after he died says it best: "Lee is a poem."

Russell Lockhart is a Jungian Analyst in private
practice in Everett, Washington. He was born in
Los Angeles in 1938. He received his B.A., M.A.
and Ph.D. at the University of Southern California.
He is the author of *Words as Eggs, Psyche Speaks* and
Dreams, Bones & the Future (with Paco Mitchell).
He has published many articles in the field of depth
psychology and in human psychophysiology. He has
taught at the University of California, Santa Bar-
bara, the University of California at Berkeley, and
the Neuropsychiatric Institute at the University of
California, Los Angeles. His research has been sup-
ported by the National Science Foundation and the
National Institute of Mental Health. He established
and was director of the Psychophysiology Laborato-
ry at Camarillo State Hospital. He was Director of
Analyst Training at the C. G. Jung Institute in Los
Angeles, and he was selected to inaugurate the C. G.
Jung Lectures in New York. He is president of RAL
Consulting, Inc., which operates an international
trading room for education in the psychology of the
financial markets and global economies. With his
wife Frankie, he edits and publishes at The Lockhart
Press. His current work focuses on the fictive pur-
pose of dreams, the commodification of desire, and a
novel entitled, *Dreams: The Final Heresy.* He welcomes feedback on this book from readers at ral@
ralockhart.com.

PERMISSIONS

In relation to books, articles, websites and all other forms of copyrighted materials, the authors have followed the fair use policy as outlined by Chicago University Press. For these copyright and fair use policies please refer to http://www.press.uchicago. edu/Misc/Chicago/copy_and_perms.pdf.

Readers are welcome to follow the above policies when referencing or quoting from the present volume. This fair use policy applies as well to readers making use of this volume's website features. Please see http://finalinterlude.com for details.

ABOUT THE PRESS

The Lockhart Press Publishes fine handmade, trade and electronic editions and provides unusual new and used books available through **The Owl Bookshop** at https://goo.gl/GhGonj. Quality items are available in psychoanalysis, Jungian psychology, philosophy, history, etymology, language, and literature, as well as the collections of The Lockhart Press, including fine handmade books and collectible editions. Current items offered are available upon request from ral@ralockhart.com. Inquiries welcome.

Typography and Design by The Lockhart Press
Editing and Proofing by Paco Mitchell

Printed by CreateSpace, an Amazon.com Company.
The paperback edition is available from
Amazon.com and other online stores.
The digital version is available for Kindle.

Made in the USA
San Bernardino, CA
13 May 2017